Mrs. Rowe's Restaurant & Bakery

74 ROWE ROAD
STAUNTON, VIRGINIA 24401

(540) 886-1833

1/2 mile east of Staunton on Route 250.
Exit 222 from 1-81 and 1-64.

First Edition 1986
Edited by Brenda Hathaway and Linda Hanna

Second Edition 1989
Edited by Brenda Hathaway

Third Edition 1991
Second Printing 1993, Third Printing 1995,
Fourth Printing 1996

Fourth Edition 1997
Edited by Brenda Hathaway
Second Printing 1999
Third Printing 2001

Printed by Marketech Direct, Inc.

Printed by Minuteman Press

Printed by Minuteman Press

Printed by Favorite Recipes® Press
P.O. Box 305142
Nashville, TN 37230
1-800-358-0560

Dear Friends,

In the ten years since the first printing of our cookbook, 50,000 copies have been sold. We have had a wonderful response from our local patrons as well as from people all over the United States. You and thousands of other travelers gave us the idea and incentive for *Mrs. Rowe's Favorite Recipes.* You've been asking for them ever since we first opened our doors in 1947 as Perk's Bar-B-Q. The collection includes the best that our kitchen has served over the years. Some recipes are original, some shared by good friends, some from long-lost sources, and some handed down from generation to generation.

Many of the recipes are contributed by family members and enjoyed by others: my daughter Brenda DiGrassie Hathaway, who managed the restaurant from 1974-1990, and my son Michael DiGrassie, who currently manages the restaurant; my daughters Linda DiGrassie Hanna and Virginia Rowe LeMasurier, who own gift shops in the area; my daughter-in-law Mary Lou DiGrassie; my sons-in-law Terry LeMasurier (a former manager of Rowe's), Dr. Steven Hanna, and Curtis Hathaway; sisters Pearl Craft

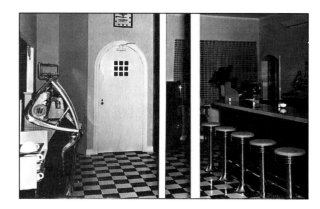

Willard Rowe

McCaleb, Virginia Craft Bowers, Bertha Craft Mays, and Estelle Craft Wright; and 11 grandchildren, who refer to me as "Moo Moo." Except for the youngest grandchildren, all the family have worked at the restaurant and contributed to its success.

Many of our recipes date from the early years when I cooked by day and waitressed at night. We had 40 seats and a five-seat counter, and the kitchen was smaller than our present guest waiting area. Today, we have a seating capacity of 250, supported by a 2,000-square-foot kitchen and storage area.

In addition to old favorites, new recipes have been added to the cookbook: "quick and easy" recipes for the cook with little

Perk's photo courtesy of John Barr.

time, recipes on the light side for the calorie conscious, pastas, and wonderful desserts for those who just love something good. Also included are a basic information section, a table of equivalents, and other helpful information.

Some of Mrs. Rowe's Restaurant recipes, such as Baked Tomatoes and Corn Pudding, should be credited to John Morris (*now deceased*), our cook and faithful employee for thirty-nine years. Vivian Obie, another faithful employee

and friend, who is in her 44th year of employment and semi-retired, contributed recipes for Bread Pudding, Rice Pudding and Apple Brown Betty.

Mrs. Rowe's Favorite Recipes is a cookbook that even the most inexperienced cook can use successfully. The recipes are simple, delicious, economical and nutritious. We hope you'll enjoy our fourth edition in celebration of our 50th anniversary (June 1997), and we invite you to visit Mrs. Rowe's Restaurant and Bakery and our beautiful Shenandoah Valley of Virginia.

Vivian Obie photo courtesy of The Daily News Leader.

April, 1997

Brenda DiGrassie Hathaway & Michael DiGrassie

This logo signifies that this recipe is a Mrs. Rowe's signature dish.

Denotes the source of the recipe.

Table of Contents

table of equivalents

note: All measurements are level

Pinch or dash = less than $1/8$ teaspoon
3 teaspoons = 1 tablespoon
2 tablespoons = 1 fluid ounce
1 jigger = $1 1/2$ fluid ounces
4 tablespoons = $1/4$ cup
5 tablespoons + 1 teaspoon = $1/3$ cup
8 tablespoons = $1/2$ cup
10 tablespoons + 2 teaspoons = $2/3$ cup
12 tablespoons = $3/4$ cup
16 tablespoons = 1 cup
1 cup = 8 fluid ounces
2 cups = 1 pint
2 pints = 1 quart
$1/3$ quart = 25.6 fluid ounces
1 quart = 32 fluid ounces
4 quarts = 1 gallon
2 gallons (dry measure) = 1 peck
4 pecks = 1 bushel

substitutions

ingredient called for	substitution
All spice	equal amount of ground cloves
Bacon	equal amount of ham
Baking powder, 1 teaspoon	$1/2$ teaspoon cream of tartar plus $1/4$ teaspoon soda
Beans, $3/4$ dried	one 16 ounce can of beans, drained and rinsed
Brown sugar, 1 cup	1 cup granulated white sugar plus 2 teaspoons molasses
Buttermilk, 1 cup	1 tablespoon vinegar or lemon juice plus sweet milk to equal 1 cup
Chocolate, 1(1-oz.) square, unsweetened	3 tablespoons cocoa plus 1 tablespoon butter or margarine
Cornstarch, 1 tablespoon	2 tablespoons flour
Currents	equal amount chopped raisins
Egg, one	2 egg yolks (for custard)
Egg, one	2 egg yolks plus 1 tablespoon water (for cookies)
Egg, 1 large	3 small eggs
Evaporated milk	Equal amount regular milk or cream
Flounder	use another flat fish such as sole, or a white fish such as cod or halibut
Flour, 1 cup, all-purpose	1 cup cake flour plus 2 tablespoons
Flour, 1 cup, cake	1 cup sifted all-purpose flour minus 2 tablespoons

substitutions, continued

ingredient called for	substitution
Flour, 1 cup, self-rising	1 cup all-purpose flour plus 1 teaspoon baking powder and $1/_2$ teaspoon salt
Garlic, 1 medium clove	$1/_2$ teaspoon minced fresh garlic or $1/_8$ teaspoon garlic powder
Ginger, 1 tablespoon fresh	use 1 teaspoon dried
Herbs, 1 tablespoon fresh	$1/_2$ teaspoon of dried herb plus 1 tablespoon chopped fresh parsley
Honey, 1 cup	$1 \ 1/_4$ cups sugar plus $1/_4$ cup liquid
Italian seasoning	combine 1 teaspoon basil, 1 tablespoon fresh or dried parsley and $1/_2$ teaspoon oregano
Ladyfingers	use equal amount sponge cake or pound cake
Leeks	use equal amounts of onions
Light cream	use equal amount of half-and-half cream
Mango	use equal amount of peach
Mascarpone cheese, 1 pound	12 ounces cream cheese mixed with 4 ounces sour cream
Mayonnaise, in salad dressings or dips	use equal amount sour cream or yogurt
Milk, 1 cup fresh	$1/_2$ cup evaporated milk plus $1/_2$ cup water
Milk, 1 cup fresh	3 to 5 tablespoons nonfat dry milk solids in 1 cup water

substitutions, <small>continued</small>

ingredient called for	substitution
Mushrooms, 1 pound	6 ounces canned mushrooms
Mustard, 1 teaspoon dry	1 tablespoon prepared mustard
Olive oil	use equal amount vegetable oil
Onion, 1 small	1 tablespoon minced dried onion or 1 teaspoon onion powder
Parsley, $1/4$ cup fresh chopped	1 tablespoon dehydrated parsley
Rabbit	use equal amount chicken
Radicchio	use equal amount red cabbage
Ricotta	use equal amount cottage cheese pureed in blender
Shallots	use equal amount chopped sweet onion
Sour cream, 1 cup commercial	1 tablespoon lemon juice plus evaporated milk to equal 1 cup; or 3 tablespoons butter plus $7/8$ cup sour milk
Sweet potato	use equal amount butternut squash
Tapioca, 1 tablespoon	$1 1/2$ tablespoons all-purpose flour
Tomatoes, 1 pound fresh	use 2 cups drained canned tomatoes
Yam	use equal amount butternut squash
Yogurt	use equal amount buttermilk or sour cream

quantities and yields

Apples	1 pound (3 medium)	3 cups sliced
Bacon	8 slices cooked	$^{1}/_{2}$ cup crumbled
Bananas	3 medium	2 cups mashed
Cabbage	1 pound head	$4^{1}/_{2}$ cups shredded
Celery	2 stalks, chopped	1 cup

Cheese,
  processed
  bleu cheese
	1 pound, shredded
	$^{1}/_{4}$ pound, crumbled
		4 cups
		$^{3}/_{4}$ to 1 cup

Chocolate morsels	6-ounce package	1 cup

NOTES:

quantities and yields, continued

Cream, whipping	1 cup ($^1/_2$ pint)	2 cups
Crumbs,		
chocolate wafers	19 wafers	1 cup fine crumbs
graham crackers	14 squares	1 cup fine crumbs
saltine crackers	28 crackers	1 cup fine crumbs
vanilla wafers	22 wafers	1 cup fine crumbs
bread	1 slice	$^1/_2$ cup soft crumbs
Dates, pitted	1 pound	3 cups chopped
	8 ounce package	$1^1/_2$ cup chopped
Eggs	5 large	1 cup
whites	8 to 11	1 cup
yolks	12 to 14	1 cup

NOTES:

quantities and yields, continued

Flour,		
all-purpose	$3^1/_2$ cups	1 pound
cake	$4^3/_4$ to 5 cups	1 pound
whole wheat	$3^1/_2$ cups unsifted	1 pound

Green Pepper	1 large	1 cup diced

Lemon	1 medium	2 to 3 tablespoons juice & 1 teaspoon grated rind

Lettuce	1 large head	6 to 7 cups torn

Lime	1 medium	$1^1/_2$ to 2 tablespoons

Macaroni	4 ounces (1-$1^1/_4$ cups)	$2^1/_4$ cups cooked

NOTES:

quantities and yields, continued

Marshmallows	11 large	1 cup
	1 large marshmallow	10 miniature
Marshmallows, miniature	8 ounces	$4^1/_2$ cups
Mushrooms	8 ounces (3 cups raw)	1 cup sliced cooked
Noodles	4 ounces ($1^1/_2$-2 cups)	$2^1/_4$ cups cooked
Nuts,		
almonds	1 pound in shell	1 cup shelled
walnuts	1 pound in shell	2 cups shelled
walnuts	$^1/_4$ pound chopped	about 1 cup
Onion	1 medium	$^1/_2$ cup chopped
	1 small	$^1/_3$ cup chopped
Orange	1 medium	$^1/_3$ cup juice and 2 tablespoons grated rind

NOTES:

quantities and yields, continued

Peaches	4 medium	2 cups sliced
Pears	4 medium	2 cups sliced
Potatoes, white	3 medium	2 cups cubed cooked or $1^3/_4$ cups mashed
sweet	3 medium	3 cups sliced
Rice	1 cup uncooked ($6^1/_2$- 7 oz.)	3-$3^1/_2$ cups cooked
Spaghetti	4 ounces	$2^1/_2$ cups cooked
Strawberries	1 quart	4 cups sliced
Sugar, brown	1 pound	$2^1/_4$ cups firmly packed
powdered	1 pound	$3^1/_2$ cups unsifted
granulated	1 pound	2 cups

cooking terms

Baste

To moisten with liquid during cooking, using a spoon or bulb blaster.

Blanch

To place in boiling water for a given amount of time and then in cold water, for the purpose of partially cooking or peeling.

Blend

To combine ingredients of different textures such as butter and sugar by a gentle mixing rather than beating.

Braise

To sear or brown in fat, then slowly cook, covered, with a minimum of liquid, on stove, in oven, crockpot or slow cooker.

Breading

A coating or dusting of flour and/or breadcrumbs used on foods that are to be fried. Beaten egg or milk may be used to help coating adhere.

Coat A Spoon

Custards and sauces which contain egg yolk or cornstarch must often cook until they are thick enough to leave a coating on a spoon, indicating their degree of doneness.

Cut And Fold

To gently combine a lighter mixture such as beaten egg whites with a heavier mixture such as a cream sauce or cake batter. To do this, place the heavier mixture over the lighter, cut down through the middle of both with a rubber spatula and draw the spatula toward you, turning the mixture over as you do so. Continue around bowl in this fashion.

cooking terms, continued

Julienne

Slice food into very long, thin matchstick strips.

Knead

To work dough by pushing it with the heel of your hand, folding it over and repeating the process until it has reached degree of smoothness indicated in recipe.

Marinate

To soak food in a liquid that will add to the flavor and/or tenderize.

Roux

A mixture of fat and flour sauteed together and then added to liquid to thicken it.

Skim

To remove fat from top of soups, stews, or pan gravies after it has risen. A spoon, bulb blaster, or a leaf of lettuce can be used but probably the easiest way to do a thorough skimming job is to chill liquid until fat solidifies at the top.

Steam

To cook in steam by placing food in a covered, perforated container over boiling water. This process preserves flavor and vitamins.

Tighten

To thicken the liquid of a soup, gravy or stew with starch such as flour or cornstarch, or with egg yolks.

cake baking tips

1. Always read the recipe through first, checking to see if you have all the ingredients called for. Assemble ingredients and utensils.

2. Use the correct size pan called for in a recipe. If the pan is too small, the batter will run over the sides and the cake will fall.

3. Prepare baking pans. Unless otherwise directed, grease the bottom and sides of the pan, sprinkle with flour, and shake the pan lightly to coat the pan with flour. Shake out any excess flour. Greasing without flouring keeps the cake from adhering to the sides of the pan and rising to full volume.

4. The most important step of cake making is proper creaming of the butter until light and soft. When adding sugar, add small amounts gradually and cream until light and fluffy and sugar cannot be felt or seen. Beat 5 minutes with a heavy-duty mixer, 6 minutes with a standard mixer, and 7 minutes with a handheld mixer.

5. Eggs give more volume when used at room temperature. Use the size eggs called for in a recipe. If small eggs are used when large eggs are called for, the batter will not be of proper consistency. When a recipe calls for folding whites into batter, the whites should be beaten until very stiff before folding, then fold, just until there are no remaining patches of white.

6. To measure dry ingredients, heap the cup or spoon, then level with a knife. When measuring flour, do not shake the cup, as you might pack in the flour and add an extra tablespoon or two of flour and alter the recipe.

cake baking tips, continued

7. Use a small amount of measured flour to dust nuts or raisins to prevent them from settling in bottom of pan during baking.

8. Preheat oven and place pans in center of oven. If the cake is placed on a rack too low in the oven, the bottom of the cake will become too brown. Keep the oven door closed until minimum baking time has elapsed. Use exact temperature in recipe; a temperature that is too low will cause the cake to fall.

9. Cake will be done if the edges have pulled away slightly from sides of the pan and the top springs back when lightly touched. Test cake for doneness with a cake tester or wooden pick. Insert it in the center of the cake and if done, it will come out clean. Underbaking results in a damp cake and sinking in the center.

10. Cool the cake in pan on a wire rack 10 to 15 minutes. Before removing from pan, run a metal spatula or knife around sides of pan. Removing too soon will also cause dampness and a sunken center. Invert onto a wire rack to remove cake from pan and invert again onto another wire rack so that the rounded top is up. Let cake cool completely.

11. Can be wrapped tightly and frozen for up to two months. Thaw without unwrapping.

appetizers

hot green pepper beef dip

2	Tbsp. butter
1	($2^1/_2$ oz. package) dried beef, chopped or broken into pieces
2	Tbsp. onion flakes
$1/_4$	cup chopped green pepper
$1/_2$	tsp. salt (don't overdo)
$1/_2$	tsp. garlic salt
$1/_4$	tsp. pepper
8	oz. cream cheese
1	cup sour cream
2	Tbsp. milk
$1/_2$	cup chopped pecans
1	Tbsp. chopped pimento
	Doritos

Melt butter and sauté beef, onion flakes, and green pepper. Season with salt, garlic salt, and pepper. Combine cream cheese, sour cream, and milk. Stir into beef mixture and add remaining ingredients. Heat until well blended. Spray 2 quart casserole with Pam. Bake at 325 degrees until bubbly.

May be made ahead of time and refrigerated. Don't bake until ready to use.

Serve with Doritos

baked crab dip yields $2^3/_4$ cups

16	oz. softened cream cheese
$1/_3$	cup mayonnaise
1	Tbsp. powdered sugar
1	Tbsp. white wine
$1/_2$	tsp. onion juice
$1/_2$	tsp. prepared mustard
$1/_4$	tsp. garlic salt
$1/_4$	tsp. salt
6	oz. canned crabmeat, drained and flaked
	chopped fresh parlsey

Combine all ingredients except crabmeat, mix well. Gently stir in crabmeat. Spoon mixture into a lightly greased 1 quart baking dish. Bake at 375 degrees for 15 minutes.

Serve warm with Melba Rounds

I usually double this because it is so good that it goes quickly.

Ginger's taco dip

8	oz. sour cream
1	16 oz. can refried beans
	dash garlic powder
	dash red pepper
2	avocados, peeled and mashed
$1/_2$	tsp. salt
$1/_4$	tsp. pepper
2	Tbsp. lemon juice
1	$3^1/_2$ oz. can chopped ripe olives
1	$4^1/_2$ oz. can chopped green chilies, drained
2	cups grated cheddar cheese
2-3	tomatoes, chopped

Mix together sour cream, refried beans, garlic powder, and red pepper. Set aside. Mix together avocados, salt, pepper, and lemon juice. Set aside. On 9 or 10 in. round serving plate, layer the ingredients as follows: sour cream-refried beans mixture, avocado mixture, ripe olives, green chilies, cheddar cheese and top with chopped tomatoes. Serve with Taco chips

May substitute $1(10^1/_2$ oz.) can of Refried Bean Dip for sour cream, refried beans, garlic powder, and red pepper.

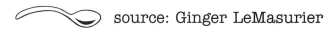 source: Ginger LeMasurier

pineapple dip-dessert topping

$^1/_2$ cup sugar
2   Tbsp. flour
1   cup pineapple juice
1   egg, beaten
1   Tbsp. margarine
8   oz. Cool Whip

Combine all ingredients and cook over medium heat. Stir constantly until smooth and thick. Cool completely and fold in Cool Whip. Refrigerate.

Serve as party dip or a dessert topping with assorted fresh fruit or berries.

 source: Mary Lou DiGrassie

pineapple pecan cheese spread

16	oz. cream cheese, softened
8	oz. crushed pineapple, drained
2	Tbsp. chopped green onion, including tops
$1/_2$	cup chopped green pepper
$1/_2$	cup chopped pecans
1	tsp. seasoned salt
1	fresh whole pineapple
2	Tbsp. chopped pecans (for topping)

Wash and dry pineapple; slice in half lengthwise, keeping leaves intact. Cut away the core, remove fruit, and reserve shell.

Cream the cream cheese, add pineapple and mix. Stir in onion, green pepper, salt and pecans. Fill scooped out fresh pineapple and sprinkle with pecans on top.

If you prefer you can roll into a large ball or 2 logs. If so, you will need additional chopped pecans.

Best served with Keebler Bacon Flavored Crackers.

This recipe was given as a Christmas present and has been enjoyed over and over again.

appetizers

chili con queso yields 2 cups

$1/3$	cup vegetable oil
3	scallions w/ tops, finely chopped
1	clove garlic, finely minced
1	Tbsp. flour
1	$5\frac{1}{2}$ oz. can evaporated milk
1	fresh tomato, chopped
1	lb. Velveeta cheese, cubed
$1/2$	cup cubed Monterey Jack cheese
3	tsp. jalapeno peppers, finely chopped*
1	large package tortilla chips

*may substitute chopped black olives

Heat oil in saucepan. Add scallions and garlic and sauté until translucent. Stir in flour and remove from heat. Slowly add evaporated milk and remaining ingredients. Return to low heat and stir until thick and smooth (about 5 minutes).

Serve warm with chips.

 source: Gwynne Elliott

pimento cheese spread

10   oz. block sharp cheddar cheese
4   oz. jar whole pimentos
3   heaping Tbsp. of mayonnaise

Let cheese soften at room temperature.

Grate cheese, add pimentos and juice. Blend well with fork. Add 3 heaping Tbsp. of mayonnaise or until soupy consistency. Refrigerate. Can add additional mayonnaise if needed when ready to serve. Will keep well in refrigerator up to 3 weeks.

Variation - may add pickle relish or chopped olives to your liking.

May serve as a sandwich spread or with crackers as an hors d'oeuvres. Suggest whole wheat bread or Wheatsworth crackers.

broccoli mushroom dip

1   package frozen, chopped broccoli
1   large onion, minced
1   stick butter or margarine
1   can cream of mushroom soup
1   can mushroom stems and pieces
1   6-oz. roll of garlic cheese
     dash of hot sauce

Cook broccoli according to package instructions. Drain and set aside. Sauté onion in butter. Add cream of mushroom soup, mushrooms and juice; stir to mix. Cut cheese into small pieces; add to mixture and stir until melted. Add hot sauce and broccoli and mix well. Serve warm in chafing dish with corn chips.

spicy baked shrimp

$^1/_2$	cup olive oil
2	Tbsp. Cajun seasoning
2	Tbsp. fresh lemon juice
2	Tbsp. chopped fresh parsley
1	Tbsp. honey
1	Tbsp. soy sauce
	pinch cayenne pepper
1	lb. uncooked large shrimp, shelled and deveined

Combine first 7 ingredients in jar and shake until well mixed. Pour into 9x13 inch baking dish; add shrimp and toss to coat. Refrigerate at least 1 hour.

Place shrimp in preheated 450 degree oven. Stir occasionally and bake until shrimp are cooked (about 10 minutes).

These spicy baked shrimp are excellent as an entree but would suggest using extra large shrimp.

 source: Brenda Hathaway

salads

salads

salad dressings

salads

greek salad makes 6 to 8 side-dish servings

5	cups torn mixed greens, such as red and green lettuce, romaine, boston, or curly endive
1	medium tomato, coarsely chopped
$1/_2$	small cucumber, sliced
$1/_2$	medium red onion, thinly sliced
1	cup kalamata olives or ripe olives
1	cup (4 oz.) crumbled feta cheese
$1/_2$	cup thinly sliced radishes
	greek vinaigrette dressing
	(see SALAD DRESSINGS for recipe)

In large salad bowl toss together the torn mixed greens, tomatoes, cucumber, onion, olives, feta cheese, and radishes. Cover and chill till serving time, at least two hours.

Just before serving, shake greek vinaigrette well to mix and pour over chilled salad. Toss gently to coat.

EXCELLENT!

tomato-feta cheese salad

$1^1/_2$ cups (7 oz.) feta cheese
$^1/_2$ cup chopped onion
$1^1/_2$ tsp. vegetable oil
1   tsp. dried oregano
6   medium tomatoes, cut into wedges
        Boston lettuce leaves

Combine cheese, onion, vegetable oil, oregano, and tomatoes; toss gently to combine. Refrigerate covered for at least two hours. Serve on Boston lettuce leaves.

cucumbers and onions

¹/₄	vinegar
2	tsp. sugar
1	tsp. vegetable oil

Stir vinegar, sugar and oil together until sugar dissolves. Set aside.

| 1 | large cucumber, thinly sliced |
| 1 | medium onion, thinly sliced and separated |

Place cucumbers and onions in serving bowl; pour oil and vinegar mixture over and refrigerate to chill.

English cucumbers are recommended when home grown ones are not available. They are seedless, have very little waste, and the flavor is very good. When selecting, look for a large firm cucumber. The price is the same, and because they seem expensive, you may as well choose a large one and get your money's worth. (Substitute ¹/₂ English cucumber for 1 regular cucumber.)

waldorf salad

3	cups diced apples
1	cup raisins
1	cup chopped celery
1	cup chopped nuts
	Miracle Whip

Mix with Miracle Whip salad dressing until well coated.

May use reduced calorie Miracle Whip. Add just before serving.

If raisins are hard, simmer in water for a few minutes to soften. Drain well and pat dry.

Use firm, juicy apples and bathe in mixture of 2 parts lemon juice and 1 part water to prevent darkening.

Walnuts or pecans are good and usually used but salted peanuts are also very good.

1 Tbsp. of sour cream, low-fat plain yogurt or whipped cream may be added to Miracle Whip to give extra body to dressing.

salads

mandarin orange garden salad

1   medium head, torn iceberg lettuce
1   head, torn Bibb lettuce
3   stalks celery, sliced
1   carrot, shredded
4   green onions, sliced
1   (11-oz.) can mandarin orange sections, drained, (save juice)
$1/_4$ cup slivered almonds, toasted

ZESTY SALAD DRESSING (see SALAD DRESSINGS for recipe except substitute 2 Tbsp. mandarin orange juice in place of 2 Tbsp. water).

Combine first six ingredients in salad bowl; cover and chill thoroughly. Just before serving, toss with Zesty Salad Dressing and sprinkle with almonds. Serves 6 to 8 side salads.

This is a traditional Christmas Eve favorite. Large salads are served accompanied by a fresh shrimp cocktail, beef tenderloin, double portions of spoonbread and Sarah's Favorite Coconut Cake.

potato salad

4	cups cooked and diced potatoes (about 7 medium potatoes)
1	medium onion, chopped
$^3/_4$	cup celery, chopped
1	medium jar chopped pimento
3	hard-boiled eggs, chopped

Mix together with cooked salad dressing (below)

cooked salad dressing

2	eggs, beaten
$^1/_2$	cup sugar
$^3/_4$	cup vinegar
1	tsp. mustard
2	Tbsp. mayonnaise

Stir eggs, sugar, and vinegar well and taste, add dash of salt and additional sugar if needed.

Place on low heat, stirring constantly until thick. Let cool. Stir mustard and mayonnaise into cooled mixture.

Pour cooled dressing over salad ingredients and mix.

Good for potato or macaroni salad.

red potato salad serves 6

10	medium red potatoes, cut into 2 inch wedges
1	pkg. Lipton onion soup mix
$^1/_4$	cup olive oil
1	tsp. crushed rosemary
1	cup torn spinach or watercress
$^1/_2$	cup sliced green onions
1	Tbsp. white vinegar

Mix potatoes, onion soup, olive oil and rosemary in a plastic bag or ziplock for best coverage. Place on sprayed cookie sheet and bake at 350 degrees for 50 minutes. Combine cooked potatoes with greens and onions. Drizzle vinegar over mixture. Good served warm or room temperature. Great for picnics because this dish keeps well and does not require refrigeration.

 source: Ginger LeMasurier

B.B.'s cole slaw

3	cups shredded cabbage
$1/_3$	cup celery, finely chopped
$1/_3$	cup grated onion
$1/_4$	cup grated carrots
$1/_4$	cup green pepper, chopped

Stir together. Add dressing (below)

dressing

$1/_4$	cup vinegar
$1/_2$	tsp. salt
$1/_3$	cup sugar
$3^1/_2$	Tbsp. mayonnaise
$1/_2$	tsp. prepared mustard

Mix vinegar, salt and sugar. Stir until dissolved. Add mayonnaise and mustard. Mix well and pour over slaw ingredients. Refrigerate if not served immediately.

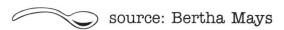 source: Bertha Mays

oriental chicken salad serves 6

$1/2$	head (about 4 cups) lettuce, shredded
3	cups cooked chicken, chopped or in strips
$1/4$	cup carrot, grated
$1/4$	cup sliced green onions
1	can water chestnuts, chopped
1	small can mandarin oranges, drained
5	cups chow mein noodles
1	Tbsp. toasted sesame seeds

ORIENTAL VINAIGRETTE DRESSING (see SALAD DRESSINGS for recipe)

Combine lettuce, chicken, carrots, onions, water chestnuts and mandarin oranges in a large salad bowl. Just before serving, add Oriental Vinaigrette Dressing and toss lightly. (Do not prepare ahead of time because the salad will wilt.) Place chow mein noodles on serving plate and top with salad mixture. Sprinkle with sesame seeds.

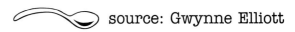 source: Gwynne Elliott

salads

baked chicken salad

4-5	cups cooked chicken, chopped
2	cups chopped celery
4	hard-boiled eggs, chopped
2	tsp. finely chopped onion
1	small jar chopped pimento
1	small can water chestnuts, chopped
2	tsp. fresh lemon juice
$3/4$	cup mayonnaise
1	tsp. salt
$1/2$	tsp. white pepper
1	can cream of chicken soup
2	cups mild cheddar cheese, grated
$2/3$	cup slivered almonds

Combine all ingredients except cheese and almonds; mix well. Lightly coat a 2 quart baking dish with a cooking spray. Place mixture in the dish, cover with cheese and sprinkle almonds over top. Cover and refrigerate overnight.

Bake covered in preheated 400 degree oven for about 30 minutes or until hot and bubbly.

May not need 2 cups of cheese but make sure that the top is covered.

Low-fat or fat-free cheese and mayonnaise could be substituted.

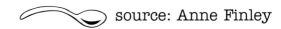 source: Anne Finley

baked chicken salad & chips

1	5 lb. hen
2	cans cream of chicken soup
3	cups chopped celery
1	medium onion, chopped
1	cup mayonnaise
8	hard boiled eggs, chopped
1	Tbsp. lemon juice
1	Tbsp. salt
	crushed potato chips

Cook the hen, cool, remove from bone and chop chicken. (Reserve and refrigerate broth for other use) Mix all ingredients; place in a buttered casserole and cover top with potato chips.

Bake in preheated 400 degree oven for 20 to 25 minutes or until hot and bubbly.

salads

crab and shrimp salad yields 6 large servings

1	lb. fresh crab meat
12	medium shrimp, cooked, peeled, and chopped
3	boiled eggs, chopped
1	stalk celery, minced
$1/_2$	medium green pepper, finely chopped
$1/_4$	cup onion, minced
1	Tbsp pickle relish
$1^1/_2$	Tbsp. lemon juice
$1/_2$	cup mayonnaise*
1	tsp. salt
1	tsp. pepper

Mix ingredients together and chill.

*Can substitute fat-free italian dressing.

salads

38

Dickie's original deviled eggs

12   large eggs
$^1/_4$ tsp. salt
$^1/_4$ tsp. white pepper
$^1/_4$ cup plus 1 Tbsp. mayonnaise
2   Tbsp. relish
1   Tbsp. relish or pickle juice
1   tsp. prepared mustard
        paprika for garnish

Boil eggs for 10 minutes, drain, pour cold water on eggs and leave until cool enough to handle. Peel and cut lengthwise.

Using a small spoon, scoop out yolks and mash with fork. Add all remaining ingredients except for paprika and blend well. Refill whites with yolk mixture and garnish by sprinkling paprika over eggs. Place in sealed container or on plate covered with plastic wrap or foil. Refrigerate until ready to eat. May be made day before serving.

Allow at least 1 egg per person (2 halves), however these deviled eggs are so good that you will want to make extra.

Sweet or dill relish can be used, but remember if using pickle juice, use the same flavor as the relish.

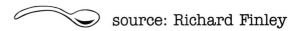

source: Richard Finley

salad dressings

sweet and sour

1	cup oil
$1/_3$	cup sugar
$1/_2$	tsp. salt
1	tsp. paprika
1	tsp. dry mustard
$1/_3$	cup vinegar
	chopped onions

Combine ingredients. Beat with rotary beater for 10 minutes and store in refrigerator. Very good on Spinach Salad.

Dijon mustard vinaigrette

$1/_3$	cup white wine vinegar
1	Tbsp. olive oil
2	tsp. Dijon-style mustard
1	tsp. sugar
$1/_2$	tsp. garlic salt
$1/_8$	tsp. black pepper

Mix well (makes about $1/_2$ cup) Very good on Spinach Salad.

bleu cheese

$1/_2$	cup mayonnaise
$1/_2$	cup sour cream
3	Tbsp. evaporated canned milk
2	Tbsp. lemon juice
$2/_3$	cup bleu cheese, crumbled
	dash of garlic powder

Mix together and let stand in refrigerator several hours before serving.

lemon-garlic

1-2   cloves garlic, crushed
        juice of 1 big lemon
$^1/_4$-$^1/_3$ cup light oil (prefer Sunlight sunflower)
1-2   Tbsp. parsley (fresh if possible)
        dash salt
1   Tbsp. sugar

Blend until well mixed.

Especially good on fresh fruit salad consisting of mixture of
greens (different kinds of lettuce other than iceberg)
Fresh orange or grapefruit sections, skinned and seeded
Seedless grapes
Sliced bananas, bathed in lemon juice 2 parts-water 1 part to
prevent darkening
Pecan halves

Toss just before serving. Increase or decrease garlic depending
on how brave you are. I love garlic so I use 2.

honey-mustard

1   cup honey
6   Tbsp. Dijon mustard
$^1/_2$-$^3/_4$ cup lemon juice

Combine all ingredients;
shake well. Adjust lemon
juice to personal tastes.

cooked salad dressing

2	eggs, beaten
$1/2$	cup sugar
$3/4$	cup vinegar
1	tsp. mustard
2	Tbsp. mayonnaise

Stir eggs, sugar and vinegar well and taste. Add dash of salt and additional sugar if needed. Place on low heat, stirring constantly until thick. Let cool. Stir mustard and mayonnaise into cooled mixture. Pour cooled dressing over salad ingredients and mix.

Good for potato or macaroni salad.

hot bacon

5	slices bacon, diced
$1/4$	cup sliced green onions
$1/2$	cup sliced fresh mushrooms
$2^{1}/_{2}$	tsp. brown sugar
$1/8$	tsp. salt
$1^{3}/_{4}$	Tbsp. vinegar
$1/8$	tsp. dry mustard
	dash of paprika

Cook bacon until crisp. Add onions and mushrooms and sauté until tender. Stirring constantly, add remaining ingredients and cook until thoroughly heated. Pour hot mixture over spinach or salad of choice and toss until coated.

oriental vinaigrette

$1/_3$ cup sesame oil (vegetable oil)
$1/_4$ cup Chinese Rice vinegar (or white wine vinegar)
1   Tbsp. sugar
2   tsp. soy sauce
$1/_2$ tsp. salt
$1/_2$ tsp. pepper
$1/_2$ tsp. ground ginger

Mix all ingredients together and refrigerate until ready to serve.

Good on Oriental Chicken Salad.

zesty salad dressing

$3/_4$ cup vegetable oil
$1/_4$ cup wine vinegar
$1/_4$ cup catsup
2   Tbsp. water
1   Tbsp. soy sauce
1   Tbsp. Worcestershire sauce
$1/_3$ cup sugar
1   clove garlic, minced
1   tsp. dried whole basil

Combine all ingredients in a jar, cover tightly, and shake well until mixed. Refrigerate until chilled. Stores well in refrigerator. Yield: $1^1/_2$ cups.

Would be good on any salad but especially good on a fruit salad (see recipe for Mandarin Orange Garden Salad)

greek vinaigrette

$^1/_3$	cup olive oil
3	Tbsp. wine vinegar
2	Tbsp. lemon juice
$1^1/_2$	tsp. snipped fresh oregano or $^1/_2$ tsp. dried oregano
1	tsp. sugar
1	small clove garlic, minced
$^1/_4$	tsp. pepper

Cover, shake well to mix. Store, covered, in the refrigerator for up to 2 weeks.

basil vinegar

1	gallon apple cider vinegar
$^1/_2$	lb. fresh basil, washed and left whole
6	whole cloves garlic
3-4	whole hot chili peppers

Pour half of vinegar into a large pan and heat until hot but not boiling. Add basil, garlic and peppers to the gallon jug or jar with remaining vinegar. Pour heated vinegar into the jar and seal with lid. Set on shelf for 2-4 weeks.

Great used with olive oil to make your own italian salad dressing or to add to taste to a commercial zesty italian dressing. Makes a great salad!

 source: Michael DiGrassie

soups

soups

white bean vegetable soup 4 main-dish servings

2   15 oz. cans cannellini beans (white kidney), rinsed and
       drained
1   tsp. olive oil
3   thin, lean slices baked ham, cut into small strips
2   medium carrots, thinly sliced
2   medium stalks of celery, diced
1   medium onion, chopped
1   medium zucchini or yellow squash, diced
$1/_2$ tsp. dried basil leaves
2   cloves garlic, chopped
$1/_4$ tsp. fresh ground pepper
1   16 oz. can stewed or diced tomatoes*
1   14 oz. can low sodium chicken broth
1   medium potato, diced
2   cups water
       grated parmesan cheese

*(if using diced tomatoes, should be chopped finer, suggest using food chopper.)

Mash half of the beans until smooth and set aside.

Heat oil in a large pot. Cook ham, celery, carrots, onions, squash, basil, garlic, and pepper in oil until vegetables are tender.

Stir in tomatoes, chicken broth, mashed beans, potatoes, and water. Bring to boil and reduce heat to low. Cover and simmer about 30 minutes. Stir in remaining beans and continue cooking until beans are heated. Check seasoning and add salt or pepper to taste. Garnish with grated parmesan cheese.

Hints: I use a 6 qt. West Bend multi-purpose cooker which is a non-stick pot and can be used on top of the stove to brown meats or vegetables. The pot sits on a base which provides the heat for slow cooking. This is a wonderful way to cook because it is so easy.

For slow cooking, follow directions down to cooking time.

Cook for about 5 hours on slow-simmer. Add remaining beans and cook another 45 minutes to an hour. Keep warm until ready to serve.

This soup is great served with Focchia, garlic bread, or crusty french bread.

soups

ham and bean soup

2	cups beans (navy, pinto or great northern) or any combination
1	Tbsp. salt
2	Tbsp. olive oil
2	medium onions, peeled and minced
3	medium cloves of garlic, peeled and minced
1	cup water
$^1/_2$	lb. ham cut into small pieces (baked or boiled ham)
16	oz. tomatoes, chopped
4	cups chicken broth
$^1/_2$	tsp. white pepper
$^1/_4$	tsp. ground cumin
	fresh black pepper
	dash hot pepper

Wash the beans. Pour into a pot, add 1 Tbsp. salt and enough cold water to cover by two inches. Heat to a boil for two minutes. Cover and let stand for one hour off the heat. Return to heat and cook the beans until tender (about one hour); drain. In a large pot add olive oil, garlic, onions and one cup water. Boil until all water has evaporated and onions are soft. Stir in all ingredients except the beans. Boil, stir and cook over medium heat until half of the liquid has evaporated. Return beans and simmer.

May use fresh tomatoes. If a hotter soup is desired, increase white pepper and cumin.

soups

vegetable soup

5	$14^1/_2$ oz. cans Swanson's vegetable broth
1	16 oz. can diced tomatoes with basil, garlic, and oregano
1	6 oz. can tomato paste
1	large onion, chopped
1	stalk celery, diced
2	carrots, diced
$^1/_2$	cup chopped cabbage
4	cups total of fresh or frozen lima beans, corn, green beans, and/or green peas
1	potato, diced
1	15 oz. can kidney or pinto beans, undrained
	cooked macaroni, optional

Mix ingredients together in large pot and season according to taste with salt, pepper and garlic powder. Bring to boil, reduce heat and simmer 2-3 hours. If using a crock pot or slow cooker, follow manufacturer's cooking directions for making soup, usually 6-8 hours.

The vegetable broth, diced tomatoes, and tomato paste are the base for the soup. Vegetables and seasonings can be varied according to preference and season. This soup is best when made with fresh vegetables.

vegetable beef soup yield 1¹/₂ gallons

1	lb. soup meat	¹/₂	cup green peppers, chopped
1	large meaty soup bone	1	cup green beans
3	qts. water	¹/₂	cup okra, sliced
1	qt. canned tomatoes	2	cups green peas
1¹/₂	cups catsup or 1(6 oz.) can tomato paste	2	cups corn
4	medium onions, chopped	1	level tsp. sugar
2	lg. carrots, chopped or sliced	1	level tsp. Lawry's seasoned salt
4	large potatoes, chopped	1	tsp. onion powder
2	stalks celery, chopped	1	tsp. garlic powder
2	cups chopped cabbage	1	tsp. Accent
			salt to taste, begin with 1 tsp.

Braise soup meat and large soup bone in large heavy stockpot. Add water, tomatoes and catsup or tomato paste to pot. Stir to mix well and bring to boil. Cook until meat is tender. Remove bone and soup meat. Chop meat and discard bone. Add all vegetables except corn and peas. Simmer 1 hour. Add peas, corn, spices and chopped meat. Simmer 10 minutes longer. Taste, add additional salt if necessary.

If soup is too thick, add additional water.
Freezes well.

chicken noodle soup serves 8

$^1/_3$ cup chopped onion
$^1/_3$ cup chopped celery
1   Tbsp. finely minced carrots
2   qts. chicken broth
8   oz. medium noodles
1   cup finely chopped cooked chicken breast

Simmer vegetables in broth until tender. Add noodles and continue to cook until noodles are done. Add chicken, heat and serve.

soups

cream of potato and bacon soup

4	cups diced potatoes
$1/_3$	cup chopped onion
$1/_3$	cup chopped celery
4	Tbsp. grated carrots
	water
6	slices bacon
4	Tbsp. bacon drippings
1	qt. milk
4	Tbsp. flour
	small amount of milk
	salt and white pepper to taste

Place vegetables and enough water to cover in large saucepan; simmer until vegetables are cooked. Meanwhile, fry bacon until very crisp; cool, crumble, and set aside. Reserve drippings.

Add bacon drippings and milk to cooked vegetable; bring to a boil and reduce heat. Mix flour with just enough milk to make a thick paste and stir into soup. Simmer until thickened; if needed, add salt and pepper at this time. Add crumbled bacon just before serving.

May omit bacon and drippings and substitute 4 Tbsp. margarine and 3 sliced fried hot dogs.

soups

potato chowder serves 6

1	Tbsp. margarine or butter
1	cup chopped onions
1	cup diced red and green peppers
6	medium potatoes, diced
3	cups chicken broth
2	tsp. dried thyme leaves
2	bay leaves
1	cup milk
10	oz. (1 pkg.) frozen corn, thawed and drained
$^1/_4$	cup chopped fresh parsley
$^1/_8$	tsp. cayenne pepper
	salt and pepper to taste

In large heavy saucepan over medium heat, melt butter. Add onions and peppers; sauté until tender. Add potatoes, broth, thyme and bay leaves; cover and cook about 15 minutes or until potatoes are tender. Remove bay leaves and discard. With slotted spoon, remove 4 cups of cooked potatoes and put into electric blender. Add milk and puree until smooth. Return to saucepan and stir in corn, parsley, and cayenne; season with salt and pepper. Cook about 10 minutes over low heat.

Garnish with grated cheddar cheese or crumbled cooked bacon and serve with crusty hot bread.

soups

old fashioned beef stew serves 12-14

$2^1/_2$	lb. boneless beef chunks, cut into $1^1/_2$ in. cubes
$^1/_4$	cup flour
2	tsp. salt
$^1/_4$	tsp. pepper
$^1/_4$	tsp. paprika
3	Tbsp. fat
1	large onion, chopped
12	small white onions
6-8	carrots, sliced
6-8	potatoes, cut into bite size pieces

Roll pieces of meat in mixture of flour, salt, pepper and paprika. Brown in fat. Add chopped onion and brown a few minutes longer. Sprinkle any remaining flour mixture over meat. Stir. Add hot water enough to just cover meat. Cover, simmer for 2 hours or until tender. Add onions, carrots and potatoes. Continue cooking 40 to 50 minutes longer or until vegetables are tender.

To vary stew, add 1 bay leaf, pinch marjoram or thyme, a minced garlic clove or 1 tsp. celery seed.

easy slow cooker beef stew serves 8

A multi-purpose cooker is recommended for this recipe because it has a non-stick 4 or 6 qt. pot which can be used on top of the stove for browning the meat, then set on a base for continued slow cooking. (West Bend is one brand). A crock pot slow cooker may also be used, but the beef and onions should be browned in a non-stick skillet or pot and transferred to the crock pot before adding other ingredients

1	Tbsp. olive oil
$1^1/_2$	lbs. lean stew beef, cut into bit size pieces
1	medium onion, chopped
$^1/_4$	cup flour
$^1/_2$	tsp. garlic salt
1	tsp. salt
$^1/_2$	tsp. white pepper
3	medium potatoes, cut into bite size pieces
3	medium carrots, sliced
1	$10^1/_2$ oz. can of beef broth
1	8 oz. can tomato sauce

Coat the bottom of a 4-qt non-stick pot with oil. Over medium heat, brown stew beef and onion. Sprinkle salt, pepper, garlic salt, and flour over browned beef-onion mixture and continue to brown for two minutes.

Add potatoes, carrots, beef broth and tomato sauce to beef-onion mixture. Cover and cook according to the directions and temperature of your cooker for stew. For the West Bend, set temperature on $3^1/_2$ and cook for 4 to 5 hours.

(Substitute for beef broth-2 pkgs. of Weight Watchers beef broth and 12-oz. of water or 1 beef bouillon cube and $1^1/_2$ cups of water.)

Great served with BB's Skillet Corn Bread and cole slaw or a green salad.

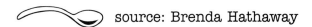 source: Brenda Hathaway

soups

turkey chili

1	Tbsp. olive oil (may substitute vegetable shortening spray to coat non-stick skillet)
1	lb. italian sweet turkey sausage
1	lg. onion, chopped
$1/_2$	cup chopped celery
1	Tbsp. minced garlic
$1/_4$	cup each of chopped red & yellow peppers
1	tsp. salt

In a large, non-stick skillet, over medium heat, sauté the above ingredients and cook until sausage is done. Drain and set aside.

In a large saucepan or a slow cooker, combine:

1	28 oz. can diced tomatoes w/ basil & oregano
1	4 oz. can mushroom pieces, drained
1	15 oz. can tomato sauce
1	26 oz. can red kidney beans, rinsed & drained
1	Tbsp. chili powder
1	Tbsp. lemon juice
$1^1/_2$	tsp. sugar
$1/_2$	tsp. cumin
2	bay leaves
1	cup water

Stir until mixed well. Add drained sausage mixture, stir, and if using the traditional cooking method, bring to a boil. Reduce heat, stir periodically, and simmer until thick, about 30 minutes. If using a slow cooker, set heat per directions for soups and sauces, and cook until thick, about 3-4 hours. When thickened, remove bay leaves and serve over rice. Garnish with shredded cheese, grated parmesan cheese, and/or chopped onions.

soups

pasta

pasta

minestrone of chard, white beans, & pasta

serves 4

$1/2$	lb. collard greens or swiss chard
1	Tbsp. olive oil
1	medium onion, chopped
2	garlic cloves, minced
1	14.5 oz. can whole tomatoes with juice, chopped
3	cups water
$1/2$	tsp. dried basil
1	19 oz. can white kidney or great northern beans, rinsed and drained
$1/2$	cup small uncooked elbow macaroni
$1/4$	cup grated parmesan or romano cheese
	pepper to taste

Thoroughly wash greens and drain. Remove stems and cut leaves into $1/2$ inch strips, set aside.

In a large heavy saucepan, heat oil over medium heat, add onion; stir and cook until tender, about 3 minutes. Stir in garlic and cook an additional minute, careful not to burn. Add tomatoes, water, and basil. Bring to a boil, reduce heat, and simmer for 10 minutes. Stir in greens and beans; return soup to a boil, stirring often until greens are wilted. Add pasta and cook about 6 to 8 minutes. Stir in grated cheese. Add pepper to taste.

Can substitute $1/2$ lb. of fresh tomatoes, skinned and coarsely chopped and $1/2$ cup tomato juice for canned tomatoes.

pasta

black bean pasta soup serves 4

1	lb. fresh spinach, coarsely chopped
2	(14 oz.) cans italian-style stewed tomatoes, chopped
3	cups water
1	tsp. dried oregano
1	tsp. basil
1	tsp. garlic powder
1	(15 oz.) can black beans, drained and rinsed
1	large zucchini, chopped
1	cup uncooked pasta shells or small macaroni
	parmesan cheese

In a 2-qt. heavy saucepan, combine first six ingredients and bring to a boil. Add black beans, chopped zucchini, and pasta. Return to a full boil and simmer until pasta is tender. When ready to serve top each bowl with parmesan cheese.

This soup makes a great evening meal when served with a salad, crusty bread, and fresh fruit.

pasta

pasta salad

1	lb. fresh pasta
1	lb. fresh mushrooms, sliced
2	cups broccoli flowerets - steamed and rinsed in cold water
6	green onions, sliced
5	oz. green olives with pimento
$^1/_2$-$^3/_4$	lb. grated fresh parmesan cheese

Cook pasta and add remaining ingredients. Add dressing and mix thoroughly.

dressing

$^1/_2$	cup red wine vinegar
2	tsp. Dijon mustard
	salt and pepper to taste
$1^1/_2$	cups olive oil
2	tsp. dried dill
2	tsp. dried basil
$^3/_4$	cup fresh snipped parsley

Whisk together vinegar, mustard, salt and pepper and olive oil. Add dill, basil and parsley. Chill for several hours.

This salad is good hot or chilled and brought to room temperature. Any pasta can be used but fettuccini, linguini or capellini is preferred. Good Season's salad dressing made with olive oil can be substituted for the dressing.

pasta

zesty pasta salad

16 oz. cooked spaghetti
$^1/_2$ bottle (2.62 oz. size) McCormick Salad Supreme Seasonings
2 medium tomatoes, chopped
1 medium green pepper, chopped
1 medium onion, chopped
1 cucumber, peeled and diced
1 bottle Zesty Italian Dressing

Combine spaghetti, seasonings and vegetables. Pour salad
dressing over all and toss to mix. Chill before serving.

pasta

pasta and greens 4 servings

1	8-oz. spaghetti, uncooked
1	(16-oz.) package of frozen greens or 1 lb. of fresh greens, cleaned and cut into $1/2$ inch strips
3	cloves of garlic, minced
3	Tbsp. olive oil
$1/2$	tsp. salt
$1/4$	tsp. freshly ground pepper
$1/2$	cup freshly grated parmesan cheese
$1/2$	jar pine nuts, toasted

Cook spaghetti according to package directions; drain and set aside.

Cook greens according to package directions or if using fresh greens, cook until tender; drain and set aside.

Sauté garlic in olive oil in skillet over medium heat until tender but not brown. Add greens, salt, and pepper to garlic oil. Stir until blended with oil and continue cooking until heated.

Combine pasta, greens, parmesan cheese and pine nuts. Garnish with additional parmesan cheese and serve immediately.

Toasting Nuts
Spread nuts in a single layer on a cookie sheet. Bake for 10 minutes at 250 degrees, or until they're light brown and you can smell them roasting.

spinach and feta stuffed jumbo shells

16   jumbo pasta shells (for filling)
1   10 oz. box frozen chopped spinach or 1 lb. fresh
            chopped spinach
$1^1/_2$ cups light ricotta cheese
10   oz. feta cheese, crumbled
$^1/_4$ cup grated parmesan cheese
$^1/_2$ tsp. garlic powder
$^1/_2$ tsp. dried oregano
2   cups prepared spaghetti sauce (marinara is very good)

Cook pasta shells according to package directions. Drain and set aside. Cook, drain by pressing all liquid from spinach, and place in mixing bowl. Combine spinach, ricotta, half of the feta cheese, parmesan cheese, garlic powder, and oregano. Fill cooked pasta shells with spinach mixture.

Place stuffed shells in a baking dish. Pour spaghetti sauce over top of shells and top with remaining feta cheese. Bake at 350 degrees for 30 minutes in conventional oven until hot and bubbly. If microwaving is preferred, cook on HIGH for 3 minutes, rotate dish, continue to cook for another 2 minutes until steaming.

If made ahead of time, stuff shells, place in baking dish, cover and refrigerate. When ready to bake, add spaghetti sauce and remaining feta cheese and bake.

pasta

penne pasta with tomatoes, bacon & feta cheese 4 large servings or 8 small portions

4 cups uncooked penne pasta
3 medium ripe tomatoes (about 1 lb.) chopped
1 medium red onion, chopped
1 garlic clove, put through a press
1 Tbsp. dried sweet basil or 1/2 cup chopped fresh basil
2 Tbsp. olive oil
2 Tbsp. Balsamic vinegar
$1/_2$ tsp. each of salt and pepper to taste
4 oz. feta cheese, crumbled
4 slices bacon
3 small zucchini
1 small onion, sliced

1 hour before
Combine tomatoes, red onion, garlic and sweet basil in a glass bowl. Add salt, pepper, vinegar, and oil. Stir to mix. Top with feta cheese, cover with plastic wrap and set aside.

Prior to serving
Cook penne pasta according to package directions; drain and set aside. Fry, drain, and crumble bacon and set aside. Use bacon drippings (or may substitute olive or vegetable oil) to lightly sauté zucchini and sliced onion.

In deep bowl, layer pasta, sautéed zucchini/onion, tomato/feta cheese. Top with crumbled bacon. Mix and serve while warm.

pasta

beef-parmesan cheese pasta serves 4

1	lb. ground beef
1	small onion, chopped
$1/2$	small green pepper, chopped
1	tsp. garlic powder
3	cups beef broth
1	can ($15^1/_2$ oz.) can Italian diced tomatoes with oregano and basil
2	cups uncooked bowtie or penne pasta
2	cups thinly sliced zucchini
$1/2$	cup freshly grated parmesan cheese

Using a large skillet, crumble and brown beef; when almost browned, add onions, green pepper and garlic powder. Continue to cook until beef is completely done. Remove from heat, pour into strainer and drain grease.

Wipe skillet clean with paper towel, add broth, tomatoes, and pasta; stir to make sure pasta is into liquid. Bring to boil, reduce heat to medium-low and cook, uncovered, for about 10 to 12 minutes. Stir frequently and add additional beef broth or water if liquid is absorbed too quickly. Add zucchini and continue to cook an additional 5 minutes or until pasta is done.

Combine drained beef and parmesan cheese with contents of skillet; stir to mix and heat through. Sprinkle with additional cheese when served if desired. Also good reheated.

 source: Brenda Hathaway

pasta

baked spaghetti makes 4 to 6 servings

$1/2$	lb. spaghetti, cooked until just tender
1	lb. ground beef
1	Tbsp. salad oil
$1/2$	cup chopped onion
$1/2$	tsp. basil leaves, crushed
$1/4$	tsp. thyme leaves, crushed
1	large garlic clove, minced
2	($10^3/_4$ oz. each) cans condensed tomato soup
1	(6 oz.) can tomato paste
2	soup cans water
$1/4$	cups grated Parmesan cheese
2	tsp. salt
$1/4$	tsp. ground black pepper
1	medium bay leaf

In large saucepan, brown beef in oil. Add onions, basil, thyme and garlic. Cook until tender. Stir in soup, tomato paste, water, $1/4$ cup cheese, salt, pepper and bay leaf. Cook over low heat 15 minutes. Stir occasionally.

Remove bay leaf from sauce. Combine sauce with spaghetti. Pour into 2 qt. shallow baking dish 12x8x2 inches. Sprinkle with remaining cheese. Bake at 350 degrees for 25 minutes or until hot. Stir before serving. Serve with additional Parmesan cheese.

pasta

feta cheese-vegetable spaghetti

4 side dish or 2 main dishes

1   Tbsp. olive oil
1   medium bermuda onion, sliced into rings
1   small red pepper, cut into strips
1   small yellow pepper, cut into strips
1   lb. fresh spinach, stems removed, cut into strips
6   small plum tomatoes, seeded and chopped
4   oz. feta cheese (more or less to taste)
8   oz. spaghetti, cooked and well drained

Cook spaghetti, drain, set aside in large bowl and keep warm.

In non-stick skillet, heat olive oil; add onions, peppers and spinach. Sauté until tender and add to spaghetti. Add tomatoes and top with feta cheese. Toss, mixing together and serve.

Options:
Substitute bacon for olive oil. Cut bacon into small pieces, fry until crisp. Remove from pan, drain on paper towel, and set aside. Sauté vegetables in 1 Tbsp. bacon drippings. Add drained bacon pieces to spaghetti mixture.

Substitute $^1/_2$ cup of parmesan cheese for feta cheese.
Other vegetables good to sauté are yellow and zucchini squash.

pasta

spaghetti with meat balls makes 6 large servings

2	Tbsp. olive oil	1	(6 oz.) can tomato paste
$1/2$	cup sliced onions	$1^1/2$	tsp. salt
1	lb. ground chuck	$1/8$	tsp. pepper
1	clove garlic, minced	1	tsp. dried sage
1	green pepper, minced	1	tsp. dried rosemary
1	(1 lb. 13 oz.) can	$1/4$	tsp. dried thyme
	tomatoes ($3^1/2$ cups)	1	bay leaf
2	(8 oz.) cans tomato sauce	1	cup water
1	(6 oz.) can whole		meatballs
	mushrooms, undrained	16	oz. spaghetti,
			cooked according to directions

Sauté onions in olive oil in large heavy pot until tender. Add meat, cook stirring often. Add garlic, green pepper, tomatoes, sauce, mushrooms, tomato paste, seasoning and water. Simmer uncovered, stirring occasionally for about $1^1/2$ to 2 hours. Sauce will become thick. Add meatballs 20 to 30 minutes before sauce is done.

meatballs

1	lb. ground chuck
$1/2$	cup pkg. dried bread crumbs
1	garlic clove, minced
2	Tbsp. fresh snipped parsley
$1/4$	cup grated Parmesan cheese
1	egg
$1/2$	tsp. salt
$1/8$	tsp. pepper
2	Tbsp. salad oil

Combine all ingredients and mix well. Shape into balls, whatever size you prefer. Add 2 Tbsp. salad oil to skillet. When very hot add meatballs and brown on all sides.

pasta

68

spaghetti with meat sauce

$1/4$	cup olive oil		1	(6 oz.) can tomato paste
$1/2$	cup minced onions		$2^1/_2$	tsp. salt
1	lb. ground chuck		$1/2$	tsp. pepper
2	cloves garlic, minced		$1/4$	tsp. sugar
2	(4 oz.) cans chopped mushrooms, undrained			pinch of fresh, dried basil or thyme
$1/4$	cup fresh snipped parsley		1	cup red wine
1	(8 oz.) can tomato sauce		$1/_2$-1	cup grated parmesan cheese
1	(1 lb. 4 oz.) can tomatoes ($2^1/_2$ cups)		16	oz. spaghetti

Heat oil in a heavy pot. Simmer onions for 5 minutes. Add meat and garlic, cook, stirring until meat has lost red color. Add mushrooms, parsley, tomato sauce, tomatoes, tomato paste, salt, pepper, sugar and basil to sauce. Stir to mix. Cover and simmer for 1 hour. Add wine; cover and simmer an additional hour.

Cook spaghetti according to directions on package. Top with sauce and sprinkle generously with parmesan cheese.

Hint: may be made ahead and refrigerated. Freezes well.
Variation: dice cheddar cheese (suggest $1/4$ pound) and toss with hot spaghetti, then add sauce and mix.

Mother usually makes a huge pot of spaghetti sauce and supplies our entire family (actually 5 families) with a source for delicious quick meals. We usually call and say "Hey Mom, got any spaghetti sauce?" Her reply is either "Come on over, I'll get it out of the freezer" or "No, but give me a couple of hours and I'll have you some."

-Brenda Hathaway

pasta

mexican spaghetti serves 6 to 8

	vegetable spray
$^1/_2$	Tbsp. olive oil
16	oz. spaghetti, uncooked
1	lb. ground beef
1	small onion, finely chopped
2	cloves garlic
1	24 oz. jar mild salsa
1	15.5 oz. can black beans, drained and rinsed
1	15.5 oz. can diced tomatoes
1	10 oz. can tomatoes and green chilies
1	$8^1/_2$ oz. can corn, drained
1	4 oz. package Four Cheese Mexican Blend
8	oz. sour cream

Prepare spaghetti according to package instructions, drain and set aside.

In large saucepan cook ground beef, onions and garlic in olive oil. Remove from pan and drain; wipe excess grease from saucepan with paper towel. Return beef mixture to saucepan and add salsa, beans, tomatoes, tomatoes and green chilies, and corn. Simmer 10 minutes.

Mix together sauce and spaghetti. Spoon into casserole dish sprayed with vegetable spray. Cover top with cheese and bake in preheated 350-degree oven for 30 minutes or until hot and bubbly. If desired, garnish with sour cream.

pasta

spaghetti casserole

$1/_4$ lb spaghetti, cooked
1   onion
1   large green pepper
1   cup pimeto stuffed olives
1   pint canned tomatoes
1   lb. fresh mushrooms, sliced lengthwise
       salt and pepper
$1/_2$ lb sharp cheese, shredded
       bread crumbs
3   Tbsp. butter
$1/_2$ cup heavy cream

Grind onion, green pepper and olives. Mix with spaghetti, adding tomatoes and mushrooms. Season to taste.

Turn into a buttered $2^1/_2$ qt. casserole. Sprinkle with cheese and crumbs. Dot with butter. Pour the cream on top.

Bake uncovered at 350 degrees for $1^1/_2$ hours.

pasta

tomato basil sauce yields 5 cups

2	Tbsp. olive oil
1	cup fresh mushrooms, sliced
2	cloves garlic, minced
1	large onion, finely chopped
1	cup diced carrots
2	tsp. salt
1	tsp. sugar
1	tsp. crushed basil
1	tsp. oregano
1	6 oz. can tomato paste
$1/8$	tsp. crushed red pepper
1	tsp. parsley flakes
$1/2$	tsp. thyme
1	28 oz. can italian tomatoes, undrained and mashed

Stir all ingredients together in a crockpot. Cook on low for 7 to 8 hours.

This is a rich sauce. A little bit goes a long way. If a thinner sauce is desired, add water. Great for pasta but another good suggestion is with chicken. Recipe as follows:

Dredge boned, skinless chicken breast in a combination of flour and parmesan cheese. Fry in a small amount of oil until golden brown. Place chicken in microwave safe dish and pour about $1/4$ cup of sauce over each breast. Top with shredded mozzarella cheese and microwave until cheese is melted. Serve on bed of pasta and sauce.

pasta

linguine with clam sauce

4	cloves garlic
2	Tbsp. flour
$^1/_2$	cup olive oil
4	$6^1/_2$ oz. can minced clams with liquid
1	8 oz. bottle all-natural clam juice
$1^1/_2$	cup chopped fresh parsley
$^1/_2$	tsp. salt
$^1/_4$	tsp. white
$^1/_4$	tsp. pepper
16	oz. linguine, uncooked

Begin to cook linguine according to package directions just before making sauce so that pasta will be ready about the time the sauce is ready; drain.

In saucepan over medium heat, saute garlic and flour in oil until golden. Gradually stir in remaining ingredients. Cook over medium-low heat, stirring constantly until sauce is thickened. Serve over pasta.

pasta

baked chicken and linguine

1	Tbsp. cooking oil
6	boneless, skinless chicken breasts
	cooking spray
1	medium onion, thinly sliced and separated into rings
1	lb. baby carrots
1	lb. fresh mushrooms, sliced
2	($10^3/_4$ oz.) cans cream of mushroom soup
10	oz. chicken broth**
$1/_4$	tsp. sage
1	lb. linguine

Coat the bottom of a large skillet with oil and place over medium-high heat. Add chicken, brown on both sides, and remove to casserole dish which has been sprayed with cooking spray.

Evenly distribute onion rings, carrots, and mushrooms over chicken breasts. Combine soup, broth, and sage; pour over casserole. Cover and bake in preheated 400 degree oven for 1 hour.

Prepare linguine according to package instructions and drain. Serve chicken breast, vegetables and sauce over pasta.

**Could substitute 10 oz. of white cooking wine for chicken broth.

 source: Michael DiGrassie

pasta

vegetables

vegetables

vegetables, continued

vegetables

corn pudding serves 6 to 8

	vegetable cooking spray
3	$16^1/_2$ oz. cans creamed style corn, drained
2	cups milk
$^3/_4$	cup flour
$^1/_2$	cup sugar
1	tsp. salt
$1^1/_2$	tsp. nutmeg
1	tsp. pure vanilla
3	eggs, beaten
$^1/_4$	cup margarine, melted

Preheat oven to 450 degrees. Spray 8x8 inch baking dish with cooking spray; set aside. Put drained corn in large mixing bowl. Combine milk, flour, and sugar and mix until smooth. Add remaining ingredients and stir until well blended; stir into corn and pour into prepared dish.

Bake until top browns, then cover with foil. Continue baking until top is set and knife inserted into center comes out clean, about 45 minutes.

Pudding can be made a day ahead, poured into an airtight container and refrigerated. Because mixture will be cold, baking time will be 55 to 60 minutes.

 source: John Morris

vegetables

baked cheese grits   6 servings

3	cups water
$3/4$	cup quick grits
$1^1/_2$	tsp. salt
4	Tbsp. butter or margarine
12	oz. grated cheddar cheese
1	tsp. minced garlic
	dash red pepper sauce
1	4 oz. can chopped green chilies, drained
2	eggs, well beaten
	vegetable spray or butter

Spray or butter a $1^1/_2$ qt. casserole dish; set aside. Preheat oven to 350 degrees.

Pour grits and salt into boiling water and cook over low heat for 3 to 5 minutes, stirring occasionally. When cooked, remove from heat, add butter and cheese, and stir until melted. Add garlic, pepper sauce and chilies. Fold in beaten eggs.

Pour into prepared dish and bake for 45 to 55 minutes, or until top is set. Let grits stand for 5 minutes before serving.

vegetables

boiled cabbage

1	medium head cabbage
3-4	Tbsp. drippings from cured salt pork or Country Ham Skins
2	cups water
1	tsp. salt
$^1/_4$	tsp. white pepper
1	tsp. sugar

Wash, dry and fry off ham skins or salt pork. Drain, reserve drippings and set aside.

Remove core from cabbage and chop coarsely. Place cabbage in a saucepan and add water. Add salt, pepper and sugar. Bring to boil. Add drippings, cover and simmer for 30 minutes or until tender.

If serving with Ham or Corn Beef, thinly slice meat and lay on top of cabbage. Simmer until meat is thoroughly heated.

vegetables

country cooked greens serves 4

2	lbs. fresh collards, turnip or mustard greens or a combination of all
2	qts. water
2	oz. salt pork, diced
1	tsp. salt
1	tsp. pepper
1	tsp. sugar

Wash greens 3 or 4 times in fresh water. Drain them each time and rinse sink to remove sand before refilling. Drain in colander; cut greens in half or smaller pieces depending on likes.

In heavy saucepan or pot, combine water, salt pork, salt, pepper and sugar. Bring to a boil. Add greens; cover, reduce heat, and simmer 1 to 2 hours or until tender. Add additional water if necessary but be sure to cook down or drain before serving.

vegetables

sautéed collards

3   lbs. collard greens
1   Tbsp. olive oil
1   cup minced onion
2   garlic cloves, minced
$^1/_2$ tsp. salt

Remove stems from collard greens. Wash, dry, and coarsely chop.
In a large pot, put about 2 inches of water and bring to a boil. Add
greens, return to a boil and cook for about 5 minutes. Drain
greens and discard water.

Heat oil in a large skillet over medium heat. Add onion and garlic
and sauté about 3 minutes or until tender. Add greens and salt
and continue to sauté until tender, about 3 to 4 minutes.

vegetables

squash casserole

2	slices bacon, fried and crumbled (reserve drippings)
6	cups squash (about 5 medium), diced
1	tsp. beef boullion
2	small onions, grated
1	green pepper, chopped
1	cup sour cream
2	eggs, beaten
$^1/_2$	cup grated sharp cheese
1	2 oz. jar pimento, drained
1	cup (or enough to cover) bread crumbs

Fry, drain, and crumble bacon, reserve drippings. Cover squash with water; add boullion and cook until tender. Drain and mash squash. Add bacon, drippings, and all remaining ingredients except bread crumbs. Stir to mix well.

Pour into a buttered or sprayed casserole dish and top with bread crumbs. Bake at 350 degrees for 50 to 60 minutes or until bubbly and browned. If deep casserole dish is used, bake 15 minutes longer.

Hints:

Buttered homemade breadcrumbs are best. If made ahead and refrigerated, cover and don't add bread crumbs until ready to bake.

On the liteside -   Substitute

• 2 Tbsp. fat-free or low fat margarine for bacon • fat-free sour cream for sour cream • low-fat cheddar cheese for cheese • omit bread crumbs • and spray casserole with vegetable spray.

 source: Brenda Hathaway

squash sauté serves 6

2	Tbsp. olive oil
1	garlic clove, minced
1	large onion, sliced and separated into rings
6	medium sized zucchini and yellow squash, thinly sliced
3	medium tomatoes, cut into wedges
1	tsp. salt
$^1/_2$	tsp. ground pepper
1	cup shredded Velveeta cheese

Coat a non-stick skillet with oil. Over medium heat, add garlic and cook until tender but not brown. Add onion and cook about a minute. Add squash and cook about 3 minutes, or until tender. Add tomatoes, salt, and pepper; stir well. Sprinkle cheese over vegetables, stirring until cheese melts. Serve immediately.

baked macaroni and cheese

2 cups uncooked macaroni
$2^{1}/_{2}$-3 cups medium sharp cheddar or Velveeta cheese, grated
$^{3}/_{4}$ cup milk
3 Tbsp. margarine

Prepare 2 cups of macaroni according to package directions. Drain.

In $1^{1}/_{2}$ quart buttered baking dish, place half of cooked macaroni. Layer with $1^{1}/_{2}$ to 2 cups grated medium sharp cheese or Velveeta. Repeat with remaining macaroni and cheese. Pour $^{3}/_{4}$ cup milk over top and dot with 2 Tbsp. margarine. Bake in preheated 350 degree oven for 20 minutes

Always spray baking dishes with cooking spray for easier cleaning.

vegetables

rice medley serves 4

2	cups rice
$2\frac{1}{2}$	cups defatted chicken broth
1	Tbsp. olive oil
1	small onion, finely chopped
2	stalks celery, finely chopped
$\frac{1}{2}$	small green pepper, chopped
$\frac{1}{2}$	small red pepper, chopped
1	cup chopped fresh mushrooms
2	oz. jar chopped pimentos

Cook rice in chicken broth according to package instructions. While rice is cooking, sauté all vegetables except pimentos in olive oil until tender. Add pimento last, stir to mix and combine vegetables with rice and serve.

Can be made ahead and reheated.

 source: Michael DiGrassie

vegetables

scalloped potatoes serves 10

1   stick margarine or butter
32 oz. bag Oreida Frozen Hash Brown Potatoes
1   tsp. salt
1   medium onion, chopped
1   can cream of chicken soup
8   oz. sour cream
2   cups shredded cheddar cheese

Melt margarine or butter in 9x13 inch baking dish; spread potatoes evenly over bottom. Mix salt, onion, soup, sour cream and 1 cup cheese; cover top of potatoes.

Cover with foil and bake 1 hour in a preheated 350 degree oven; uncover, cover top with remaining 1 cup of cheese and bake an additional 15 minutes or until cheese melts.

Potatoes can be prepared ahead of time and refrigerated but allow additional baking time.

Reduced fat substitutions can be made for the cream of chicken soup, cheddar cheese, sour cream. Reduce margarine to $^1/_2$ stick.

Good, good good!

 source: Brenda Schuler

vegetables

scalloped cheese potatoes serves 4 to 6

3	Tbsp. butter
2	Tbsp. flour
1	tsp. salt
$1/4$	tsp. pepper
3	cups milk
1	cup shredded sharp cheddar cheese
6	medium potatoes, pared, thinly sliced and parboiled
1	medium onion, thinly sliced and separated into rings

Melt butter in saucepan over low heat. Blend in flour, salt and pepper. Add milk all at once. Cook quickly, stirring constantly until mixture thickens and bubbles. Remove from heat immediately and add cheese. Stir until cheese melts.

Place half the potatoes in a buttered 2 qt. casserole; cover with half the onion and half the sauce. Repeat layers.

Cover and bake at 350 degrees for 45 minutes. Uncover and continue baking until top is brown.

vegetables

candied yams

1	(29 oz.) can yams, drained (save syrup)
$1/_2$	tsp. nutmeg
$1/_4$	tsp. cinnamon
$1/_2$	tsp. vanilla
$1/_2$	tsp. lemon juice
$3/_4$	cup brown sugar
$1/_4$	cup white sugar
3	Tbsp. cornstarch
1	stick margarine, plus enough to butter baking dish

Place yams in a buttered baking dish. Pour yam syrup into saucepan and add all ingredients except the cornstarch and margarine. Cook until it reaches a boil then add margarine and stir in cornstarch. Pour over yams and bake at 350 for 30 minutes.

You may want to prepare a double recipe and mash leftover yams and sauce. Place them in a buttered baking dish and heat well in 325 oven.

sweet potato casserole serves 8

        vegetable cooking spray
1   29 oz. can sweet potatoes
1   17 oz. can sweet potatoes
$1/_2$ cup firmly packed dark brown sugar
$1/_2$ cup applesauce
$1/_2$ stick butter or margarine, melted
2   tsp. vanilla extract
6   oz. flaked coconut
10   oz. of large marshmallows

Spray casserole dish with cooking spray; set aside. Drain and mash sweet potatoes; combine with sugar, applesauce, butter, and vanilla extract. Pour into casserole dish and bake in preheated 350 degree for about 25 minutes or until hot. Remove from oven; sprinkle with coconut and arrange marshmallows on top. Return to oven and bake until marshmallows are golden brown.

vegetables

sweet potato soufflé serves 8

3   cups mashed sweet potatoes
1   cup sugar
$1/_2$ tsp. salt
2   eggs
$1/_3$ stick margarine or butter, melted
$1/_2$ cup milk
1   tsp. vanilla

Preheat oven to 350 degrees. Grease casserole dish with butter.

Mix all ingredients and pour into prepared dish. Cover with topping.

1   cup brown sugar
$1/_3$ cup flour
1   cup chopped nuts
$1/_3$ stick margarine, softened

Mix thoroughly and evenly distribute on top of sweet potato mixture. Bake in preheated oven at 350 degrees for 35 minutes.

 source: Betty Fox

vegetables

baked tomatoes

1   Tbsp. cornstarch
4   cups diced tomatoes, drained (reserve 2 cups juice)
$1/_2$ cup sugar
1   stick butter
        dash salt
2   Tbsp. butter
3   cups homemade coarsely ground breadcrumbs

Mix cornstarch with just enough juice to make a smooth paste, pour remaining juice in saucepan and stir in cornstarch mixture. Simmer over low heat, stirring occasionally until thickened; juice will have a glossy appearance.

Heat tomatoes, sugar, salt, and butter until sugar and butter melt. Add thickened juice, stir and simmer for a few minutes.

Mix bread crumbs with enough melted butter to moisten. Put a very thin layer of crumbs to barely cover the bottom of a buttered casserole dish, then pour tomatoes, and top with remaining bread crumbs. Bake in preheated 400 degree oven until bubbly and browned (usually 20 minutes)

*4 $14^1/_2$ oz. cans diced tomatoes will equal 4 cups of tomatoes. If additional juice is needed to reserve juice to equal 2 cups, add regular tomato juice.

 source: John Morris

vegetables

scalloped tomatoes

1	small onion, chopped
$^1/_2$	cup chopped green pepper
1	Tbsp. extra virgin olive oil
2	28 oz. cans peeled diced tomatoes, drained
	(save 1 cup of juice)
	salt and pepper to taste
1	tsp. sugar
$1^1/_2$	cup toasted bread cubes
$1^1/_2$	cup grated parmesan or cheddar cheese

Preheat oven to 350 degrees; prepare casserole dish by buttering or spraying with vegetable spray; set aside.

Sauté onions and green pepper in olive oil. Combine tomatoes, 1 cup juice, onion, green pepper, sugar, bread cubes and 1 cup of cheese. Pour into prepared casserole dish. Cover top with remaining cheese. Bake uncovered for 30 minutes or until hot and bubbly.

vegetables

fried green tomatoes   serves 4

4   medium green tomatoes, sliced $^1/_2$ inch thick
        sugar, salt, pepper
1   cup milk
        cracker or corn meal
        bacon drippings or oil

Sprinkle tomatoes lightly with sugar, salt and pepper. Set aside
for about 10 minutes. Tomatoes should become moist with a
liquid formation however there may not be enough moisture so
that meal will stick to the tomatoes in order to form a crust. If
that is the case, dip tomatoes into milk, making sure to dredge
each slice well.

Fry in 2 inches of bacon drippings or oil in heavy skillet over
medium-high heat. Don't crowd the skillet and allow space
between slices. This method allows the grease to sear the
tomatoes, forming a crunchy crust, rather than absorb the
grease, resulting in soggy tomatoes. Carefully turning only once
with tongs, fry until golden brown on both sides. Stand them up
to drain on a paper towel.

vegetables

pickled beets

1	16 oz. can beets
$^1/_2$	cup sugar
$^1/_2$	cup vinegar
	pinch of salt

Mix well and chill before serving

 green beans

2	lbs. fresh greens <u>or</u>
4	lbs. canned green beans
2	qt. water
1	country ham hock
	salt and pepper to taste
$^1/_4$	tsp. sugar

If using fresh beans, string, snap, and wash. If using canned beans, drain and thoroughly rinse.

Place ham hock and water in large pot, cover and cook for 20 minutes. Add beans, cover and cook over medium heat for 30 minutes longer. Check seasoning, add salt and pepper to taste if desired. Remove ham hock, trim fat, chop meat and return to pot. Simmer additional 10 minutes.

vegetables

pinto beans

1   lb. pinto beans
1   small ham hock
      salt and pepper

Sort, pick and wash beans. Place in large pot, cover with water and add ham hock. Bring to a boil and simmer until beans are tender (about 2 hours). Add additional water if needed. Taste broth and add salt and pepper if needed. Simmer until broth is thick.

Great with corn bread and cucumbers and onions.

vegetables

white beans

such as great northern, large limas, or navy beans

1   lb. dried beans
2   oz. salt pork or a small ham hock
6   cups water
1   large yellow onion, chopped
1   tsp. white pepper
1   tsp. salt

Look at beans in small batches and discard pebbles or beans with holes in them. Wash beans and drain. Put beans in a large heavy pot or dutch oven, cover with water, and bring to a boil. Boil for two minutes, remove from heat, and let beans stand for 2 hours.

Rinse salt pork; make slices through pork but not through rind. Drain beans and discard water. Fill heavy pot to half full with water, add pork, beans and remaining ingredients.

Cover, bring to boil, reduce heat, and simmer about 2 to $2^1/_2$ hours until tender. Add more hot water if necessary to keep beans barely covered.

vegetables

baked beans serves 6

2	slices bacon, diced
$1/3$	cup minced onions
$1/3$	cup chopped green peppers
1	(16 oz.) can pork and beans
1	garlic clove, minced
$1/4$	cup catsup
3	Tbsp. brown sugar
1	Tbsp. Worcestershire sauce
$1/2$	tsp. salt
$1/4$	tsp. dry mustard
	dash pepper

Cook bacon until almost done; add onions and green peppers and sauté until bacon is done.

Combine all ingredients in a lightly greased casserole dish. Bake at 425 degrees for 35 to 40 minutes or until bubbly.

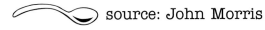 source: John Morris

vegetables

black-eyed peas and greens serves 4

1	lb. fresh greens (kale, collards, or turnip greens) or 10 oz. pkg. frozen chopped turnip greens, (I have never found frozen kale or collards)
1	Tbsp. olive oil
1	Tbsp. chopped garlic
	pinch of ground red pepper
1	15 oz. can black eye peas, drained and rinsed
1	Tbsp. white vinegar (or more to taste)

If using frozen greens, cook according to directions, drain and set aside.

If using fresh greens, wash and drain. Pull the leaves from the stems and chop into about 1" pieces. Place in large pot with about 2" water, cover, bring to boil and cook until tender. Drain and set aside.

Coat the bottom of a large non-stick skillet with oil. Add garlic and cook over low heat for about 2 minutes or until it begins to sizzle. Add the peas and red pepper, stir to mix, and cook for about 2 minutes. Over low heat, stir in drained cooked greens, mix well and cook until thoroughly heated. Add vinegar and serve.

I usually double the recipe so that I have leftovers. This dish is great reheated.

 source: Brenda Hathaway

vegetables

fried green apples

6   cups small unpeeled green apples
4   Tbsp. butter
$1^1/_2$ cups sugar

Wash, core and quarter apples. Melt butter in skillet. Add apples and sugar. Cover and cook until done, stirring occasionally.

Great for breakfast with sausage gravy and buttermilk biscuits or with fried pork chops and B.B.'s Alabama Biscuits.
(see biscuit recipe)

 # baked apples

8   medium apples, quartered
$1/_4$ stick butter or margarine, melted
$1^1/_2$ cups sugar
$1/_3$ cup water
1   tsp. nutmeg
$1/_2$ tsp. cinnamon
$1/_4$ cup water

Place apples in buttered baking dish. Sprinkle sugar, nutmeg, and cinnamon on top. Pour water over top. Spoon butter over all. Bake uncovered in 325 degree oven for 30 to 45 minutes. Cooking time will depend on the type of apples used.

vegetables

mushrooms and bacon in wine sauce

8   slices bacon
4   Tbsp. butter
$1/_8$ tsp. rosemary
1   lb. fresh mushrooms, sliced
2   Tbsp. flour
1   cup dry white wine

Fry bacon crisp, drain, and crumble. Set aside. Leave drippings in pan.

Add butter and rosemary to bacon drippings in skillet and heat until bubbly. Add mushrooms, reduce heat, and cook, stirring for about 4 minutes until mushrooms are tender. Add crumbled bacon and cook 1 minute more. Remove mushrooms and bacon and set aside.

Add flour to skillet; stir constantly to brown flour (about 1 minute). Gradually add wine and cook, stirring constantly until sauce is smooth and thick. Remove from heat and stir in bacon and mushrooms. Serve immediately.

Excellent but rich!
Could be served on dry toast points or in a puffed pastry shell as a main dish and will serve 4. Serves 8 as a vegetable.

vegetables

main dishes

main dishes, continued

main dishes, continued

southern fried chicken

1	2 to 2$^1/_2$ lb. fryer, disjointed
1	cup all purpose flour
$^1/_2$	tsp. salt
$^1/_2$	tsp. white pepper
2	cups buttermilk
2	cups solid shortening (enough to have fat 1$^1/_2$ to 2 inches deep

Combine flour, salt and pepper and put in paper bag. Coat chicken pieces in buttermilk, then shake in bag until well covered with seasoned flour.

Melt shortening in heavy skillet until very hot. Add chicken to pan, reduce to medium heat and cook until underside is golden brown, approximately 15 minutes. Turn and cook until other side is brown, then reduce heat to low, cover and cook 10 minutes longer.

If using a large chicken, may have to increase cooking time. Don't crowd chicken in the pan, have space between each piece.

All the grandchildren come to Moo Moo's house for fried chicken, macaroni and cheese, gravy and biscuits.

skillet gravy

4   Tbsp. drippings
$^1/_2$ cup flour
1   tsp. salt or to taste
2   cups half milk and half water (for thick gravy)
3   cups half milk and half water (for thin gravy)

After frying chicken or meat, pour drippings from skillet. Return 4 Tbsp. drippings to skillet; add flour and salt. Brown over medium heat, loosening brown crusty bits from skillet. Stir until smooth and browned.

After browning, remove from heat and stir in half and half mixture. Return to heat, stir and simmer until well mixed and begins to thicken.

If serving gravy at table as a side dish, make a thicker gravy. If preparing a dish to be baked, prepare a thinner gravy because it will thicken as it bakes.

country style chicken

1	(2 to 2$^1/_2$ lb.) fryer, disjointed
1	cup all purpose flour
2	cups buttermilk
$^1/_2$	tsp. salt
$^1/_2$	tsp. pepper (freshly ground if possible)
2	cups solid shortening (enough to have fat 1$^1/_2$ to 2 inches deep)

Follow procedure for Southern Fried Chicken except do not cook as long since additional cooking is required in oven.

Place chicken pieces in greased baking dish. Make skillet gravy per directions except double recipe and make gravy thinner. The gravy will thicken during baking.

Cover and place in preheated 325 oven and bake for 45 minutes.

old fashioned chicken & dumplings

1	large hen	$1^1/_2$	cups milk
$1^1/_2$	tsp. salt	$^1/_2$	cup flour
1	large onion, chopped		
	enough water to cover		

Cut chicken into serving pieces. Place chicken, salt and water in large pot. Cook slowly for 45 minutes or until tender, add onions and cook for 15 minutes. Remove chicken to platter, cover and keep warm.

Strain broth, pour 1 quart in saucepan for gravy and return 2 quarts to pot for cooking dumplings. (If additional is needed, add canned broth.)

Add milk to broth in saucepan and heat; mix small amount of milk to flour to make a paste. Remove broth from heat, whisk in paste, and return to low heat. Stirring occasionally, simmer until thickened. If not thick enough, repeat thickening process.

dumplings

2	cups flour	1	egg, beaten
2	tsp. baking powder	2	Tbsp. Crisco
1	tsp. salt		just enough milk to
			make a stiff dough

Sift together flour, baking powder and salt. Add egg, Crisco and milk. Roll out on floured board $^1/_4$ in. thick, cut into 2x3 inch pieces. Add to hot chicken broth and cook 10-15 minutes.

dressing

8	cups coarse homemade bread crumbs
2	medium onions, minced
4	stalks celery, finely chopped
3	tsp. sage
2	tsp. salt
1	tsp. white pepper
$1\frac{1}{2}$	cups chicken broth

Mix together and spoon into greased baking dish. Bake at 350 degrees for 30 minutes or until brown.

May use any type of broth depending on preference.

 ## oven-broiled barbecue chicken

$2\frac{3}{4}$	lb. broiling chicken, halved
	melted butter
	salt and pepper to taste
8	oz. Mrs. Rowe's Beef Rib Sauce

Place chicken in baking dish, brush well with butter. Add salt and pepper. Place in 400 degree oven and bake for 20 minutes. Remove from oven, reduce temp to 350 degrees, brush with Beef Rib Sauce and return to oven for 15 min. Adapt amount of sauce to personal preference.

grilled cornish hens serves 4

$1/4$	cup olive oil
$1/2$	cup fresh lime juice
1	Tbsp. finely minced garlic
3	tsp. ground cumin
$1/2$	tsp. ground cinnamon
$1/2$	tsp. salt
	freshly ground pepper to taste
4	cornish hens (1 lb. each)*

*If using a larger hen, $1^3/4$ lb. size, serve half hen per serving. To butterfly, cut the hens along the back. Trim away the backbone and discard. Cut off the wing tips. Gently flatten with hand until hen lies flat on surface.

Combine all marinade ingredients in small jar and set aside.

Butterfly hens, wash well and dry. Put in dish or plastic bag and cover with marinade. Refrigerate and marinade at least 6 hours or better still, overnight.

Grill on well-oiled rack over medium coals for 10 minutes. Baste, turn and grill another 10 minutes. If using larger hens, cooking requirement is about 30 minutes or until juice runs clear when the thickest part of hen is pierced.

This technique can be used with any marinade.

chicken or turkey pot pie serves 8

8	cups chicken or turkey broth
6	cups cubed chicken or turkey
$1/4$	cup minced onions
2	cups corn
2	cups green peas
2	cups diced carrots
$1/2$	cup flour
	water
	salt and pepper to taste
3	hard boiled eggs, chopped
	10 unbaked biscuits or unbaked pie pastry
	melted butter

Combine first 5 ingredients in large saucepan. Bring to a boil, reduce heat and simmer for 15 minutes. Stir often to prevent sticking. Prepare thickening by adding just enough water to flour to make a smooth thick paste. Slowly add to chicken mixture, stirring constantly. Season with salt and pepper if desired. Add eggs last.

Pour into a greased 13x9 inch baking dish and cover with biscuits or pastry $1/3$ inch thick. Press pastry against side of the dish to seal. Cut several slits in top to vent steam.

Bake at 425 degrees for 15 minutes or until brown. Remove from oven and brush with melted butter.

chicken with mushrooms and sour cream

2	broiler-fryer chickens, $2^1/_2$ lbs., cut up
	salt and pepper
$^1/_4$	cup butter
2	cups whole small white onions, fresh or unthawed frozen
1	clove of garlic, finely minced
1	Tbsp. paprika
16	oz. canned tomatoes, chopped
2	4 oz. cans button mushrooms, undrained
$^1/_2$	cup sour cream

Season chicken pieces with salt and pepper. Over medium heat, melt butter in large skillet. Brown chicken on all sides. Remove to platter and set aside.

Add onions to drippings remaining in skillet. Cook and stir frequently for 2 minutes; stir in garlic and paprika and cook for 1 minute. Add tomatoes and mushrooms with liquid. Return chicken pieces to skillet, cover, and bringing to a boil. Reduce heat, simmer 20 to 25 minutes or until chicken is tender.

Remove chicken to platter and keep warm. Skim fat from sauce and add sour cream. Return to low heat, stir constantly and cook only until sauce is hot. Pour over chicken and serve with butter noodles.

roast turkey and gravy

1	14-16 lb. turkey**
1	Tbsp. salt
	melted butter or vegetable oil
2	cups water

Remove and set aside neck, giblets, and liver. Wash and dry
turkey. Thoroughly rub salt inside cavity; brush turkey with
butter or oil. If cavity opening has band of skin across, push
drumsticks underneath; otherwise, tie legs to tail. Lift wingtips
up and over back and tuck under turkey.

Place breast side up on roaster rack. Insert meat thermometer
in the meaty part of the thigh, making sure not to touch bone.
Add water and bake at 325 degrees until the meat thermometer
reads 185 degrees, (see roasting chart, helpful information
section). If turkey starts browning too much, cover loosely with
aluminum foil.

When two-thirds through baking, according to chart, release
band of skin holding the legs so that the heat can reach the
inside of thighs. Turkey is done when drumsticks can easily be
moved up and down or twisted out of joint. Remove from pan,
keep warm and let stand 20 minutes before carving.

Pan juice can be combined with giblet broth to make a delicious
gravy.

**If using a different size turkey, adjust amount of salt and water.

turkey gravy

Put neck, giblets, and liver in saucepan with 4 cups of chicken broth. Canned chicken broth can be used or broth can be made using 4 chicken bouillion cubes or $1^1/_2$ Tbsp. chicken soup base mixed with 4 cups of boiling water. Add 1 whole small onion and 1 chopped stalk celery. Cover and simmer slowly about $1/_2$ hour. Do not add seasonings; the chicken broth will have yielded enough.

Strain broth; dice giblets and liver to be used in gravy. Set aside. Measure combined pan juices with giblet broth, pour into saucepan and heat. For 3 cups of broth, mix 1 cup water and $1^1/_2$ cup all-purpose flour to make a smooth paste. (Stir a little water into flour until smooth, then stir in remaining water.)

Remove broth from heat and slowly stir flour mixture into broth. Return to heat and cook, stirring constantly. When gravy is bubbling, add chopped giblets and liver, reduce heat and simmer about 5 minutes, stirring occasionally.

creamed turkey on biscuits   serves 8

3   cups cubed turkey or chicken
4   cups turkey or chicken broth
1   cup frozen corn
1   cups frozen peas and carrots
$^1/_4$ cup minced onions
$^1/_4$ cup minced celery
3   Tbsp. flour
        water
        salt and pepper
2   hard cooked eggs, chopped
8   buttermilk biscuits

See recipe for buttermilk biscuits and bake so that they are just
out of the oven and piping hot when creamed turkey is ready to be
served.

Combine first 6 ingredients in large saucepan. Cook on low heat
for 15 minutes; stir often to prevent sticking.

In small bowl, add just enough water to flour to make a smooth
thick paste. Slowly add to turkey mixture, stirring constantly. Add
salt and pepper as desired. Stir in chopped eggs and serve over hot
split biscuits.

chicken fried steak serves 6

6	4 oz. portions cube steak
6	eggs
1	cup buttermilk
1	tsp. tabasco sauce
1	tsp. Worcestershire sauce
	salt to taste
	flour (enough to flour meat)
$1/_2$	cup cooking oil
1	qt. milk
$1/_2$	cup buttermilk
$1/_2$	cup butter, melted
$1/_2$	cup flour
2	tsp. black pepper

Make an egg wash by mixing together eggs, 1 cup buttermilk, tabasco sauce, worcestershire sauce, and salt.

Lightly flour each portion of steak, dip into egg wash, and then into flour again to coat the steaks. Heat cooking oil in skillet and fry steaks until golden brown. Ladle gravy over steaks and serve.

gravy instructions
Combine milk and $1/_2$ cup buttermilk and heat in double boiler. Combine butter and flour to make a roux. Using a wire whisk, add roux to hot milk mixture. Add salt and pepper to taste and let simmer 30 to 40 minutes or until thick.

 source: Chad Coffey Chef, Mrs. Rowe's

country style steak serves 6

6	4 oz. pieces cubed steak (prefer sirloin)
$1/_2$	cup flour
$1/_2$	tsp. salt
$1/_2$	tsp. pepper
$1/_2$	cup shortening

Mix flour, salt and pepper. Flour meat, melt shortening in skillet until hot, then add floured meat. Brown on each side 5 to 8 minutes. Remove meat and put in baking dish.

Pour gravy over meat and bake uncovered in preheated oven at 325 degrees for 45 minutes.

This is a family favorite. We like it with mashed potatoes, green beans, cucumbers and onions and, of course, with Alabama biscuits.

gravy

4	Tbsp. drippings
$1/_2$	cup flour
1	tsp. salt or to taste
3	cups half milk and water

Pour drippings from skillet. Return 4 Tbsp. of drippings to skillet and add $1/_2$ cup flour and 1 tsp. salt (left from coating steak plus additional if needed.) Brown over medium heat, loosening brown crusty bits from skillet. Stir until smooth. After browning, remove from heat and stir in half and half mixture. Return to heat; stir and simmer until well mixed but thin. Will thicken as it bakes in the oven.

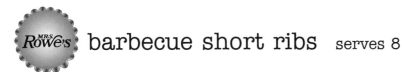 # barbecue short ribs serves 8

8	lb. beef short ribs
$1/_4$	cup worcestershire sauce
1	cup A-1 Sauce
3	dashes tabasco sauce
2	Tbsp. garlic powder
	black pepper to taste
$2^1/_2$	Tbsp. salt
	vegetable spray
1	pt. Mrs. Rowe's Beef Rib Sauce

Place ribs and seasonings in large pot, cover with water, bring to a boil; reduce heat and simmer for 1 hour. Drain broth (excellent for gravy or soup). Place short ribs in a large baking dish which has been sprayed with vegetable spray. Pour Mrs. Rowe's Beef Rib Sauce over ribs and cover loosely with foil. Bake at 350 degrees for $1^1/_4$ hour or until meat is tender.

pot roast with vegetables & gravy serves 8

1	4 lb. chuck roast
1	tsp. garlic powder
1	tsp. seasoned salt
1	tsp. pepper
3	Tbsp. vegetable oil
2	cups water
3	medium onions, peeled and quartered
6	medium potatoes, peeled and cut in half
6	medium carrots, peeled and cut in half
2	Tbsp. flour
$^1/_2$	cup or enough water to make a paste
	salt and pepper to taste

Wash, pat dry and rub seasoning into meat. Add oil to heavy pot or dutch oven. Add seasoned meat and sear on both sides until brown. Pour water around meat and place onions on top of meat. Cover tightly and simmer $1^1/_2$ to 2 hours or until meat is very tender. Add potatoes and carrots, cover tightly, and simmer an additional 30 minutes.

Remove from heat, transfer roast and vegetables to serving platter and keep warm. Stir water into flour to make paste. Measure broth and enough water to make 3 cups. Return broth to pot, add flour paste to broth and whisk until smooth. Cook over medium heat until gravy thickens, whisking constantly. Season to taste with salt and pepper.

pot gravy

1	qt. broth
2	Tbsp. flour
$1/2$	cup water
	salt and pepper

This basic recipe can be used with any type broth and depending on the type of broth used, gravy may not need additional salt and pepper.

In a small bowl, make thickening by adding just enough water to flour to make a smooth, thick paste. Bring broth to a boil, add salt and pepper to taste if needed. Remove from heat, whisk flour paste into the hot broth. Return to heat, continue to cook and whisk constantly until gravy is smooth and thick. If gravy seems too thick, slowly add water until gravy is desired consistency.

For table gravy, make a thicker gravy. If adding to a dish to be baked, such as baked stuffed pork chop, make a thinner consistency because the gravy will thicken as the dish is baked.

stuffed green peppers

	vegetable cooking spray
6	medium green peppers
1	lb. ground beef
$1/_3$	chopped celery
$1/_3$	chopped onions
1	tsp. salt
1	tsp. mustard
$1/_4$	cup catsup
1	egg, beaten
1	tsp. Texas Pete
1	tsp. A-1 sauce
1	tsp. worchestershire sauce
1	tsp. white pepper
$1/_2$	cup bread crumbs
$1/_2$	tsp. garlic salt

Cut off tops of peppers and remove seeds. Parboil pepper cups in small amount of salted water for 5 minutes; drain. Mix next 13 ingredients together, divide into 6 portions and stuff peppers. Prepare sauce. Pour approximately $1/_4$ cup of sauce into a baking dish which has been sprayed with vegetable shortening. Place stuffed peppers in dish. Pour 1 to $1^1/^2$ cups sauce on top. Bake in preheated 375 degree oven for 45 to 50 minutes. Spoon on additional sauce if needed.

sauce makes enough for 12 peppers

$1/_2$	sugar
1	Tbsp. Texas-pete
1	Tbsp. A-1 sauce
1	Tbsp. worcestershire sauce
42	oz. tomato juice
1	Tbsp. salt
2	tsp. white pepper
$1/_2$	cup catsup
2	level Tbsp. cornstarch
4	oz. tomato juice

Mix first 8 ingredients together and heat. Make thickening using cornstarch and tomato juice; add to mixture, stirring constantly. Simmer until thickened.

spicy baked meatloaf serves 8

	vegetable cooking spray
2	lb.s ground beef
1	cup Italian bread crumbs
1	medium onion, finely chopped
$1/2$	medium green pepper, chopped
2	cups hot salsa
1	Tbsp. worcestershire sauce
	dash tabasco sauce
1	tsp. salt
$1/2$	tsp. pepper
1	tsp. garlic powder

Preheat oven to 400 degrees. Prepare baking dish with cooking spray; set aside. Mix all ingredients together and form into one large loaf or two small loaves. Put into baking dish and bake for 1 hour.

 source: Brenda Hathaway

shepherd's pie serves 8

2	lb. hamburger
1	med. onion, chopped
$1/_4$	cup A-1 sauce
2	dashes Texas Pete
1	tsp. garlic powder
	salt and pepper to taste
2	cups peas and carrots to taste
4	cups cold mashed potatoes
1	med. onion, minced
2	cups grated cheddar cheese

Brown hamburger and onion; add A-1 sauce, Texas Pete, and garlic powder. Add salt and pepper to taste. Simmer for 5 minutes.

Drain hamburger to remove excess grease and spoon into grease casserole dish. Mix mashed potatoes and onion together. Layer the hamburger with peas and carrots, mashed potatoes, and top with cheese. Cover with foil and bake in a 350 degree oven for 45 minutes or cheese is melted but not overcooked.

To reduce fat, use very lean hamburger or ground turkey. Prepare mashed potatoes with butter flavored granules or sprinkles and skim milk, and use 1 cup of reduced fat cheddar cheese.

liver and onions serves 4

1	lb. sliced beef liver
1	cup flour
	salt and pepper
2	Tbsp. butter or margarine
$1/_4$	cup butter or margarine
$2^1/_2$	Tbsp. flour
1	cup beef broth
1	Tbsp. butter
2	large onions, peeled and thinly sliced

Season liver with salt and pepper; Dredge well in flour. Melt 2 Tbsp. butter in large skillet and cook liver until brown. Remove from skillet and set aside.

Over medium heat, melt $1/_4$ cup butter in skillet; add flour to melted butter, stirring constantly for about 1 minute. Add beef broth; cook, stirring constantly, until thickened and bubbly. Return liver to gravy, cover and simmer 10 minutes. In small skillet, melt 1 Tbsp. butter; add onions and sauté until tender.

When liver is done transfer to platter and cover with sautéed onions; serve gravy on side. Completed dinner menu with fluffy mashed potatoes, fresh green beans, B.B.'s cole slaw, and hot buttered rolls.

zucchini casserole serves 6 to 8

1	28 oz. can tomatoes, drained and save juice
2	packages Lipton onion soup mix
2	cups tomato juice (in addition to saved juice)
4-6	oz. spaghetti
	water
1	lb. ground beef
1	Tbsp. olive oil
2	onions, sliced
1	small green pepper, chopped
3-4	small zucchini or yellow squash, sliced
1/4	cup fresh parsley
1	cup freshly grated parmesan cheese

Drain tomatoes and set aside. Pour juice, onion soup, and water in a pot large enough to cook spaghetti according to directions on package. When cooked, drain spaghetti but save 1 cup liquid to be used later.

Over medium heat, brown ground beef in non-stick skillet; drain and discard grease. Heat olive oil in skillet; Add onions, green pepper and squash and cook until tender. Combine with spaghetti, 1 cup of reserved liquid, drained tomatoes, parsley, and $^1/_2$ cup parmesan cheese. Pour into a casserole dish, cover with $^1/_2$ cup (or more to liking) of parmesan cheese. Bake in preheated 375 degree oven for 30 minutes or until bubbly.

 source: Janet Ferguson

brunch casserole serves 4

3	cups frozen shredded hash browned potatoes
1	cup shredded monterey jack cheese
2	oz. chopped green chilies
1	cup diced cooked ham
$1/4$	cup sliced green onion
4	well-beaten eggs
1	12 oz. can evaporated milk
$1/4$	tsp. pepper
$1/2$	tsp. salt

Grease a 8-in. square baking dish. Arrange potatoes evenly in bottom. Sprinkle cheese, chilies, ham, and green onions over top.

Combine eggs, milk, pepper and salt and pour over the potato mixture. Cover and refrigerate overnight or at least four hours before baking. Bake uncovered, in preheated 350 degree oven for 55 to 60 minutes or until set in center. Let stand several minutes before serving.

Serve with fresh melon or assorted fresh fruit, assorted muffins or banana nut bread.

baked marinated pork tenderloin serves 6

$1/_2$	cup peanut oil	2	Tbsp. worcestershire
$1/_3$	cup soy sauce	2	cloves garlic, crushed
$1/_4$	cup red wine vinegar	1	Tbsp. of parsley
3	Tbsp. lemon juice	1	Tbsp. dry mustard
$1^1/_2$	tsp. fresh ground pepper		

2   ($^3/_4$ pound) fresh pork tenderloin (2 to a package)

Combine ingredients for marinade in jar with a top; shake well. (If planning to cook meat the day before serving, double marinade recipe and reserve $^3/_4$ cup of marinade to pour over meat before reheating.)

Trim fat and membrane from tenderloin, wash, pat dry, and put into zip-lock plastic bag. Pour marinade into bag and seal. Refrigerate and marinade for 24 hours, turning at intervals.

When ready to bake, preheat oven to 325 degrees. Remove meat and place on a rack in a shallow roasting pan. Discard marinade. Bake for 45 minutes or until meat thermometer inserted into thickest part of the meat registers 160 degrees. Remove meat from oven and let stand before slicing into thin slices.

This may be cooked the day before serving, sliced, covered and refrigerated. When ready to serve, place meat in a microwavable dish, pour saved marinade over meat, cover with plastic wrap and microwave until hot.

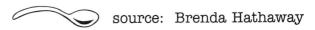 source: Brenda Hathaway

baked pork tenderloin with carrots and mushrooms serves 4

4	portions pork tenderloin, 1 in. thick, butterflied
	salt and pepper
1	Tbsp. olive oil or vegetable oil
1	lb. fresh mushrooms, stems removed, sliced or whole
1	lb. fesh baby carrots
1	$10^3/_4$ oz. can cream of mushroom soup
1	can water
$^1/_2$	tsp. sage
$^1/_2$	cup sour cream

Wash, pat dry, and remove excess fat from tenderloin. Lightly salt and pepper. In non-stick skillet over medium heat, brown tenderloin in olive oil and place in baking dish. Cover top with mushrooms and carrots. Mix together cream of mushroom soup, water, sage, and sour cream. Pour over tenderloin, cover and bake in preheated 400 degree oven for 1 hour.

Add rice to your meal and spoon the gravy over the rice for a tasty accompaniment. Complete the meal with a green vegetable, bread, and fresh fruit for dessert.

Lessen the fat in this recipe by using Campbell's Healthy Request Soup and low-fat or fat-free sour cream. Trim all fat from meat and brown in non-stick skillet, using a cooking spray and omitting the oil.

 source: Michael DiGrassie

baked pork tenderloin   serves 4

8   pieces tenderloin, $^1/_2$ inch thick
$^1/_2$ cup flour
$^1/_2$ tsp. salt
$^1/_2$ tsp. pepper
$^1/_2$ cup shortening

Mix flour, salt, and pepper. Melt shortening. Flour meat and add
to hot shortening. Brown well on both sides, remove, drain, and
place in baking dish. Cover with a thin gravy and bake at 350
degrees for 1 hour.

gravy

4   Tbsp. drippings
$^1/_2$ cup flour
1   tsp. salt to taste
3   cups half milk and half water

Pour drippings from skillet. Return 4 Tbsp. of drippings to skillet
and add flour and salt. Brown over medium heat, loosening brown
crusty bits from skillet. Stir until smooth.

After browning, remove from heat and stir in milk and water.
Return to heat. Stir and simmer until well mixed but thin. Will
thicken as it bakes in the oven.

baked stuffed pork chops

4	pork chops, $1^1/_2$ inches thick
1	cup flour
1	tsp. salt
$^1/_3$	tsp. white pepper
1	egg, well beaten
1	Tbsp. prepared mustard
$^3/_4$	cup milk
1	cup dressing
1	cup cooking oil

Prepare pork chop by cutting slit along fat side and into chop to form a pocket. Combine flour, salt and pepper. Prepare egg wash by mixing egg, mustard, and milk.

Using $^1/_4$ cup dressing, stuff tightly into pocket and press fatty edges together to close.

Dip each chop into egg wash, then flour. In very hot oil, fry until golden brown. Remove, drain and place in large casserole dish. Cover with thin gravy. Cover with foil and bake at 325 degrees for $1^1/_2$ hours. Remove foil and bake uncovered an additional 30 minutes.

dressing

3	cups bread crumbs
1	small onion, minced
2	stalks celery, finely chopped
$^1/_2$	tsp, salt
	white pepper
1	tsp. sage
	broth, any kind

Mix together and add only enough broth to hold crumbs together. Do not make dressing too wet.

pork chops with apples   serves 4

4	center-cut boneless loin pork chops
$1/_4$	tsp. salt
$1/_4$	tsp. freshly ground pepper
1	Tbsp. cooking oil
4	large cooking apples, peeled, cored and quartered
1	cup apple juice
$1/_4$	cup brown sugar

Trim all excess fat from pork chops and season with salt and pepper. Coat the bottom of a large non-stick skillet with oil and heat over medium-high heat. Add chops, brown on both sides, remove to a plate and set aside.

Add the apples to skillet and cook until lightly browned. Remove apples to plate. (The apples must be handled gently with tongs so that they do not tear up when turning and removing to the plate.)

Pour the apples juice into the skillet, increase heat to high and boil until the juice is reduced by half. Return the chops to the skillet and cover with the apples. Sprinkle brown sugar over the apples, cover loosely and cook over medium-low heat until chops are done, about 20 minutes. Remove the chops and apples to a platter. If the pan juices are not thick, boil, stirring constantly, until thick and syrupy, 1 to 2 minutes. Spoon over the pork and apples and serve.

Vegetable spray can be substituted for cooking oil to cut fat.
A flavorful substitute for apple juice is $1/_2$ cup of bourbon. The alcohol cooks out but the flavor remains.

baked pork chops, sweet potatoes & apples

6	center cut boneless pork chops, (approx. $1^1/_2$ lbs.)
	salt & pepper to season
1	Tbsp. oil
1	29 oz. can cut sweet potatoes, drained and rinsed
3	cups firm apples (granny smith) cored and sliced
3	Tbsp. packed brown sugar
$^1/_2$	cup apple juice
$^1/_2$	cup water

Preheat oven to 350 degrees. Coat a large non-stick skillet with cooking oil. Season chops with salt and pepper and brown on both sides. While chops are browning, arrange sweet potatoes and sliced apples in a 2 qt. casserole dish and sprinkle brown sugar evenly on top. Pour apple juice over and lay browned pork chops on top. Set aside.

Add water to skillet and over high heat, stir to loosen crusty particles. Boil for two minutes and pour over casserole. Bake covered for 1 hour, remove cover and bake an additional $^1/_2$ hour until chops are tender.

to reduce fat and calories:
• buy a leaner, thinner boneless pork chop and remove all fat
• substitute a vegetable cooking spray to brown chops
• substitute granulated brown sugar substitute for part of brown sugar

Virginia country ham with red eye gravy

serves 6

6    $^1/_4$ inch thick slices Virginia country ham
1   cup strong coffee

Cut off and discard rind from ham. Trim off fat, leaving a small amount of fat around edge; reserve excess fat. Cut small gashes in fat to keep from curling. Scrape ham with dull edge of knife, wash, and pat dry.

Place trimmed excess fat pieces in a heavy skillet and cook over medium-low heat. Add ham and cook until brown, turning several times. Remove to a heated platter and keep in warm oven or warming drawer. Discard fat pieces.

Add coffee to skillet and bring to boil over medium heat, stirring to loosen clinging particles. Reduce heat and simmer 4 to 5 minutes, or until slightly thickened, stirring frequently. Spoon gravy over ham and serve with grits, fried apples and buttermilk biscuits.

pork barbecue

4   lb. fresh Boston Butts
1   pt. Mrs. Rowe's Pork Barbecue Sauce

Remove excess fat and cut into 2x2 inch cubes. Cover with water, bring to boil and simmer for $1^1/_2$ hr. Remove from heat, drain, and chop according to desired consistency. Add enough Pork Barbecue Sauce to meat to make very moist. Place in container, seal and allow to set overnight. Keep refrigerated.

Great on bun with cole slaw or serve as entree with Baked Beans, slaw, and corn bread. The pork broth would make good gravy for the Baked Stuffed Pork Chops.

country ham hocks and cabbage

4   medium to large country ham hocks
       hot water, enough to cover
1   medium hard head of cabbage, chopped

Wash ham hocks and place in large deep pot. Cover with hot water and simmer until meat is almost done. (approx. $1^1/_2$ hrs.)

Add cabbage and cook covered for 15 to 20 minutes longer or until cabbage is tender. After cooking, taste cabbage and add salt and pepper if needed.

ham and cabbage serves 4

1	medium size hard head of cabbage, chopped
1	tsp. salt
$^1/_2$	tsp. pepper
2	cups water
$^1/_2$	lb. thin sliced baked western ham

Put chopped cabbage in large saucepan; season with salt and pepper. Add water and cook covered low heat for about 20 minutes or until cabbage is tender. Lay ham on top of cabbage and cook an additional 5 minutes or until cabbage has cooked down and no water remains.

Suggest serving with pinto beans, cucumbers and onions, and corn bread.

pan roasted spareribs

$^1/_4$ cup extra virgin olive oil
1   chopped onions
4   lbs. spareribs, trimmed and cut into individual ribs
1   cup coarsely chopped carrots
1   cup coarsely chopped celery
2   cups canned italian peeled, chopped tomatoes with juice
         salt and pepper

In a large deep non-stick skillet or pan large enough to hold ribs in one or two layers, heat oil over medium heat. Add onions and cook until tender; add spareribs and brown on both sides, turning occasionally.

Add carrots and celery and cook for about 3 minutes. Add tomatoes and salt and pepper to taste. Cover ribs and simmer for about $1^1/_2$ hours until tender. If using a lid with a vent, leave the vent open. If using a solid lid, partially cover. Check ribs occasionally to see if they have cooked down and need water added to prevent sticking. If so add about $^1/_2$ cup each time. When ribs are done, if juice is too thin, uncover and boil over higher heat until juice becomes thicker. Serve with fluffy mashed potatoes.

breaded fried catfish serves 10-12

5	lbs. catfish fillets
6	eggs
$1/2$	gallon milk
$1/2$	cup hot sauce
$1/2$	cup A-1 sauce
$1/4$	cup worcestershire sauce
$1^1/2$	Tbsp. lemon juice
1	12 oz. box breading mix
2	Tbsp. white pepper
3	Tbsp. salt
	vegetable oil for frying

If catfish fillets are not small, cut into strips 2-2$1/2$ inches wide. Prepare batter by combining eggs, milk, hot sauce, A-1, worcestershire sauce, and lemon juice. Combine breading mix, pepper, and salt. Heat oil. Fish may be deep fried or pan fried. If pan fried, have oil $1/2$ inch deep. Dip fillets in batter, dredge in breading and fry in hot oil until golden brown. Drain on paper towel and keep warm until ready to serve.

Great with baked beans, cole slaw, and hush puppies.

 source: Karl Craig Chef, Mrs. Rowe's

salmon cakes with white sauce serves 4

1   15$^1/_2$ oz. can pink salmon, drained
$^1/_2$ cup grated onion
1   egg, beaten
$^1/_2$ cup finely ground bread crumbs
$^1/_4$ tsp. white pepper
$^1/_4$ cup celery, finely minced
1   Tbsp. parsley flakes
1   Tbsp. lemon juice
$^1/_2$ cup each of bread crumbs and flour for breading
       shortening for frying

Remove skin and bones from salmon, flake with a fork. Mix all ingredients together except for breading and form into eight round flat salmon cakes. Coat with bread crumb and flour mixture and fry over medium high heat until golden brown. Drain and serve.

white sauce makes 1 cup
3   Tbsp. butter
4   Tbsp. flour
$^1/_4$ tsp. salt
1   cup milk
       white pepper

Melt butter in sauce pan over low heat. Blend in flour, salt, and dash of pepper. Add milk, cook quickly, stirring constantly, until mixture is thick and bubble.

 source: Karl Craig   Chef, Mrs. Rowe's

marinated tuna steak

4	tuna steaks, $^1/_2$ thick	
$^1/_4$	cup olive oil	
$^1/_4$	cup margarine, melted	
$^1/_4$	cup soy sauce	
1	Tbsp. lemon juice	
1	garlic clove, minced	

<u>red wine marinade</u>

1	cup red wine (sweet wine)
$^1/_4$	cup soy sauce
$^1/_4$	cup catsup
$^1/_4$	cup olive oil
2	Tbsp. brown sugar
2	cloves garlic, minced

Place fish in casserole dish. Mix marinade by combining all ingredients in a jar and shake vigorously. Pour over tuna; cover and refrigerate for 6 to 8 hours. Turn steaks over once.

Cooking technique is personal preference. <u>Grill</u> over medium hot coals approximately 8 to 10 minutes, turning once, and basting with remaining marinade. Cook until fish flakes easily. (Suggest using a well greased wire grill basket.)

<u>Broil</u> in preheated broiler. Place steaks on greased, unheated rack of broiler pan and broil 4 inches from heat 4 to 6 minutes, or until fish flakes with fork, brushing occasionally with marinade. Do not need to turn.

<u>Pan Grill</u> using no-stick surface griddle or skillet. Heat (do not need to use oil). Cook 4 minutes on each side, brushing occasionally with marinade. Check for doneness.

 source: Red wine marinade, Georgette L. Keene, Franklin, Virginia

sausage gravy

1	lb. sausage patties
$^1/_4$	cup sausage drippings
$^3/_4$	cup flour
1	tsp. salt
1	tsp. white pepper
3	cups half milk and water

Fry sausage, remove from skillet and set aside to drain on paper towel. Remove sausage drippings and save $^1/_4$ cup to be returned to skillet for making gravy. Heat drippings, add flour, salt and pepper, and brown over medium heat. After browning, remove from heat and stir in milk mixture. Return to heat, stir and simmer until thickened. Crumble sausage and add to gravy.

Must serve with Buttermilk Biscuits & Fried Green Apples (see recipes.)

 source: Vivian Obie, Baker, Mrs. Rowe's

 ## chipped beef gravy

2	pkg. (6 oz.) dried beef	Chop dried beef. Melt butter in
$^1/_4$	cup butter or margarine	saucepan over low heat; add and
$^1/_4$	cup flour	blend flour, salt, and pepper. Add
$^1/_2$	tsp. salt	milk, stirring constantly; add dried
$^1/_8$	tsp. white pepper	beef and cook until mixture is thick
2	cups milk	and bubbles. Serve over biscuits or
		toast.

breakfast tenderloin gravy   serves 6

$^1/_2$	cup shortening
$^1/_2$	cup flour
$^1/_2$	tsp. salt
$^1/_2$	tsp. white pepper
8	pieces tenderloin, $^1/_2$ inch thick

Melt shortening over medium high; mix flour, salt and pepper and coat meat well. Add to hot shortening and brown on both sides. Remove, drain, (reserve 4 Tbsp. drippings for gravy) and place in baking dish. Cover with a thin gravy and bake at 350 degrees for at least $1^1/_2$ hours or until tenderloin is so tender that it falls apart. Using a large spoon or knife, cut tenderloin into small pieces; stir to evenly distribute in gravy and spoon over hot biscuits. This makes a very hearty breakfast and is very good served with Fried Green Apples, (see recipe in vegetable section.)

gravy

4	Tbsp. drippings
$^1/_2$	cup flour
1	tsp. salt or to taste
3	cups half milk and half water

Return drippings to skillet and add flour and salt. Brown over medium heat, loosening brown crusty bits from skillet. Stir until smooth.

After browning flour, remove from heat and stir in milk and water. Return to heat; stir and simmer until well mixed but thin. Will thicken as it bakes in the oven.

on the liteside

on the liteside

Regular recipes can be altered by substituting low-fat or fat-free for regular in recipes calling for sour cream, cheese, cream cheese, yogurt, and margarine. Skim milk and skim evaporated milk are a good substitute and even low or fat-free sweetened condensed milk which will lighten those fat grams and calories in a dessert. A cooking spray, such as Pam, is good for browning meat and spraying casserole and baking dishes.

Fat-free chicken broth is good for making soup, seasoning vegetables, rice and pasta, and to make gravy. There are several good canned broths or use homemade but skim fat from broth.

Fat-free italian dressing is very good to marinade chicken, beef and vegetables before grilling. If using oil is must, use olive oil or a vegetable oil but use less.

Butter flavored sprinkles are a wonderful seasoning for potatoes, vegetables, and fish. Vegetable cooking spray can also be substituted for oil in certain recipes.

Two small kitchen appliances which are wonderful for cooking with less fat are the Betty Crocker Steam-n-Grill Express and the West Bend 6 Quart Slow Cooker. The cookbook which accompanies the steam grill is self explanatory but this is a wonderful quick way to grill your food low-fat and tasty. The slow cooker, which is an oblong non-stick pot with a removal rack, sits on a griddle heating base. The cooker is especially good because meat can be browned and cooked on the rack with the juices draining away from the meat. The glass dome top allows a view of the contents without removing the top and losing heat.

creamy corn and zucchini soup serves 8 to 10

4	14.5 oz.-ounce cans fat-free chicken broth*
3	cups diced zucchini
$1/_2$	cup chopped onion
6	cups fresh or frozen corn
1	tsp. salt
$1/_2$	tsp. white pepper

Combine broth with zucchini and onion in large saucepan; bring to boil, cover, reduce heat and simmer for about 8 minutes. Stir in corn, salt, and pepper and continue to simmer covered for about 5 minutes.

Place about 3 cups in blender and process until almost smooth. Repeat process with remaining soup. The corn puree makes the soup thick without using cream.

*If using canned chicken broth, fat-free is available. If using homemade, let cool and remove fat from top.

on the liteside

on the
liteside

zucchini-potato soup   serves 8 to 10

2	medium size thinly sliced leeks, white part only
1	garlic clove, minced or 1 tsp. prepared minced garlic
1	tsp. salt or to taste
$1/4$	tsp. white pepper
2	$14^1/_2$ oz. cans fat-free vegetable broth
2	$14^1/_2$ oz. cans fat-free chicken broth
3	medium baking potatoes, peeled and diced
4	medium zucchini, diced
4	medium yellow squash, finely diced
2	Tbsp. fresh chives or green onions, minced
1	Tbsp. fresh lemon juice

In a large saucepan, combine leeks, garlic, salt, pepper and one can of broth. Simmer, covered until soft. Add potatoes and remaining broth; cover, bring to boil, and simmer for ten minutes. Add zucchini and squash, cover, and simmer until tender; cool and puree in a blender until smooth. Return to pot, stir in chives and lemon juice. Reheat and serve.

potato breakfast casserole serves 6

vegetable spray
3   cups frozen shredded hash browned potatoes
$3/4$ cup shredded low-fat cheddar cheese (3 oz.)
1   cup diced canadian bacon
$1/4$ cup sliced green onion
1   cup egg substitute
1   12 oz. can evaporated skim milk
$1/4$ tsp. white pepper
$1/8$ tsp. salt

Spray a 2 qt. baking dish with vegetable spray. Evenly distribute potatoes in bottom of dish. Sprinkle with cheese, bacon, and onions over top.

Combine egg substitute, milk, pepper and salt. Pour this mixture over potato mixture. Cover and refrigerate overnight. In a preheated 350 degree oven, bake uncovered for 60 minutes or until center is set. Let stand a few minutes before serving.

Serve with fresh fruit and light biscuits (see recipe)

on the liteside

sausage-cheese breakfast casserole serves 6

	vegetable spray
$3/_4$	lb. ground pork, crumbled
$3/_4$	tsp. dried italian seasoning
2	cloves garlic, minced
1	cup skim milk
16	oz. frozen egg substitute, thawed
$1/_4$	cup (1 oz.) shredded low fat cheddar cheese
3	green onions, finely chopped
$3/_4$	tsp. dry mustard
$1/_4$	tsp. salt
$1/_4$	tsp. ground red pepper
6	slices light (low fat) white bread, cut into $1/_2$ inch cubes

Coat a non-stick skillet with cooking spray and heat over medium heat until hot. Add crumbled pork, italian seasoning, and garlic to skillet and cook over medium heat until meat is browned. Drain and pat dry with paper towels; set aside.

Stir together milk, egg substitute, cheese, onions, mustard, salt and pepper. Add pork and bread cubes, stir enough to blend. Coat a 11x7x2 inch baking dish with cooking spray; add mixture, cover and refrigerate overnight.

Bake in a preheated 350 degree oven, uncovered for 50 minutes or until lightly browned and set. Let stand for 10 minutes before serving.

on the liteside

broccoli and chicken casserole serves 6

	vegetable coating
4	oz. medium noodles
$2^1/_2$	cups chopped chicken or turkey
1	10 oz. package frozen chopped broccoli, thawed
$^1/_2$	cup sliced green onions
1	$10^3/_4$ oz. can low-fat cream of mushroom soup
$^1/_2$	cup skim milk
$^1/_2$	cup shredded swiss cheese (2 oz.)
1	tsp. dried basil, crushed
$^1/_8$	tsp. pepper
	paprika

Cook noodles according to package directions. Drain well.

Combine noodles, chicken or turkey, broccoli, and onions. Mix together soup, milk, cheese, basil, and pepper and stir into noodle mixture. Pour into a 2 qt. casserole which has been sprayed with vegetable spray.

Bake, uncovered, in a preheated 350 degree oven for 40 to 50 minutes or until hot and bubbly. Sprinkle with paprika.

on the liteside

light biscuits yield 1 dozen

2	cups all purpose flour
3	tsp. baking powder
$1/_4$	tsp. baking soda
$1/_2$	tsp. salt
$1/_4$	cup low-fat margarine
$1/_2$	cup plain fat-free yogurt
1	tsp. honey

Combine first four ingredients in bowl; cut in margarine with fork or pastry blender until mixture looks like coarse meal. Add yogurt and honey and stir just until ingredients are moistened.

Turn dough out onto lightly floured surface and knead several times.

Roll dough to a $1/_2$ inch thickness and cut into rounds using a biscuit cutter or juice glass. Transfer biscuits to an ungreased baking sheet. Bake at 425 degrees until golden brown, about 10 to 12 minutes.

mashed potatoes serves 8

A basic mashed potatoes recipe uses potatoes, whole milk, and butter. To convert to low fat, substitute skim milk for whole milk; fat free sour cream for butter, and enhance the flavor with minced scallions, roasted garlic, or fresh herbs.

2	lbs. potatoes, peeled and quartered
$2/3$	cup skim milk
1	tsp. salt
2	Tbsp. fat-free sour cream
$1/4$	tsp. freshly ground pepper
$1/4$	cup finely chopped fresh chives (optional)
$1/4$	cup chopped fresh basil (optional)
$1/4$	cup finely chopped scallions (optional)

Cook potatoes in a large pot of water over high heat until tender, about 20 to 25 minutes. Drain well and place in mixing bowl. Beat potatoes with an electric mixer until partially mashed. Add the salt, milk, and sour cream and beat until smooth. Add pepper and optional seasoning to taste. Set aside and keep warm until ready to serve.

This basic recipe can be modified to make feta mashed potatoes which are delicious! Reduce the skim milk to $1/4$ cup, add 3 Tbsp. of feta cheese, eliminate the optional seasoning and add $1/2$ tsp. dried oregano. All the other ingredients remain the same.

on the liteside

scalloped potatoes

	vegetable coating
$^1/_2$	stick reduced fat margarine
1	Tbsp. butter-flavored sprinkles
32	oz. bag of frozen hash brown potatoes
1	tsp. salt
1	medium onion, finely chopped
1	can reduced-fat cream of chicken soup
2	cups shredded low-fat cheddar cheese
1	cup fat-free sour cream

Spray 9x13 inch baking dish with vegetable coating. Add margarine and melt; Add butter sprinkles and spread potatoes evenly over bottom.

Mix together salt, onion, soup, 1 cup cheese, and sour cream. Spread evenly over potatoes. Cover with foil and bake in preheated 350 degree oven for 1 hour. Uncover, cover top of casserole with remaining cheese and bake an additional 15 to 20 minutes or until cheese has melted and casserole is hot and bubbly.

Butter Buds are a good butter flavored sprinkle.

oven fries

5   medium potatoes, peeled and cut into strips
       vegetable cooking spray
       salt

Preheat oven to 450 degrees. Spray baking sheet with cooking spray. Prepare potatoes, wash, and pat dry. Arrange potatoes in single layer on baking sheet. Spray with cooking spray and sprinkle salt, according to taste. Bake for 35 minutes or until golden brown.

oven browned new potatoes

small new potatoes (allow 3 per person)
cooking spray
seasonings

Wash and leaving skin on, quarter potatoes. Boil until done; drain and set aside. Spray baking sheet with cooking spray. Pour drained potatoes on the sprayed baking sheet and lightly spray potatoes with cooking spray. Add seasonings and place in preheated 400 degree oven. Bake until browned, about 10 to 15 minutes. Suggest seasoning with salt for breakfast potatoes. If preparing lunch or dinner, use garlic powder or salt, rosemary, Mrs. Dash's seasoning, or other seasoning of choice.

on the liteside

potato salad serves 6

4	medium potatoes, peeled and cubed
1	cup chopped celery
$1/_4$	cup finely chopped onion
2	Tbsp. sweet pickle relish
$1/_2$	cup low-fat or fat-free mayonnaise
$1/_2$	cup plain low-fat or fat-free yogurt
2	tsp. prepared mustard
$1/_2$	tsp. salt
1	hard cooked egg, chopped

Cook potatoes until tender; drain, cool, and place in a large bowl. Stir in celery, onion, and relish.

Combine mayonnaise, yogurt, mustard, and salt. Pour over potato mixture; toss gently to coat potatoes. Fold in chopped egg. Cover and chill several hours before serving.

I prefer this dish with low-fat rather than fat-free mayo and yogurt, but it depends on individual preference. Try it both ways and see which you prefer.

baked cheese grits serves 6

3	cups water
$^3/_4$	cup quick grits
$1^1/_2$	tsp. salt
2	Tbsp. low fat-reduced calorie margarine
1	Tbsp. butter flavored sprinkles (Butter Buds is good)
1	cup grated low fat cheddar cheese
1	tsp. minced fresh garlic
	dash tabasco
1	4 oz. can chopped green chilies
3	egg whites, well beaten or egg substitute to equal 2 eggs

Cook grits and salt in water according to box directions for 5 minutes. Remove from heat, add margarine, butter sprinkles, and cheese; stir until melted. Add garlic, tabasco, and chilies. Fold in egg whites or stir in egg substitute.

Pour into a baking dish which has been sprayed with non-stick vegetable coating and bake in preheated 350 degree oven for about 45 to 55 minutes. Bake until knife inserted into center comes out clean. Let stand 5 minutes before serving.

on the liteside

fresh green beans

2   lbs. fresh green beans
2   qts. water
     salt and pepper to taste
     pinch of sugar
     vegetable cooking spray

Cook fresh green beans in water, using salt, pepper, and a pinch of sugar for seasoning. Can add a small amount of chopped onion for additional flavoring. Near the end of cooking when the beans have cooked down and very little water remains, spray the top generously with vegetable cooking spray (such as Pam). Continue to cook until no water remains.

This cooking technique is also good for cooking squash and greens, omitting sugar. For peas, green limas, peas and carrots, season with butter sprinkles, such as Molly McButter or Butter Buds.

on the liteside

154

steamed squash sauté

1   small yellow squash, sliced
1   small zucchini, sliced
1   small onion, chopped
1   Tbsp. low calorie margarine
         Mrs. Dash's seasoning

Steam squash until medium crunchy. Melt margarine in a non-stick skillet and sauté onion sprinkled with seasoning. Pour steamed vegetables into skillet with onions and sauté until well mixed. Serve immediately.

This is especially good for the diet conscious with Broiled Fish.

tomato-basil pasta serves 2

2   large ripe tomatoes, chopped
1   small white onion, chopped
$^1/_4$ lb. fresh basil, chopped
$^1/_2$ tsp, garlic powder
1   Tbsp. olive oil

About 2 hours or more before serving, prepare tomato-basil mixture. Mix tomatoes, onions and basil together. Sprinkle garlic powder over. Add olive oil and mix. Cover and let set for several hours at room temperature. When ready to serve, prepare pasta according to directions for serving size desired and top with tomato-basil mixture.

May want to adjust quantity according to personal preference. This may be served hot or cold.

pasta salad serves 8

1	8 oz. pkg. spaghetti, uncooked
1	4 oz. can sliced ripe olives, drained
1	cup frozen english or early peas, thawed
1	medium red pepper, chopped
1	small zucchini, chopped
$1/2$	small bermuda (purple) onion, chopped
$1/4$	cup fat-free parmesan cheese
$1/2$	cup fat free or low-fat mayonnaise
$1/2$	cup low fat or fat free italian dressing
1	tsp. dried parsley flakes
$1/2$	tsp. dried dill weed
$1/2$	tsp. ground pepper

Cook spaghetti according to package directions; drain. Rinse with cold water and drain.

Combine olives, peas, red pepper, zucchini, onion, and parmesan cheese in large enough bowl to mix. Add spaghetti and mix well.

In a small jar, combine mayonnaise and remaining ingredients. Shake vigorously to mix. Add to pasta mix and stir well. Cover and chill.

This is a very good salad and easy to make, but I haven't developed a taste for the fat free parmesan cheese. Using Kraft grated 100% parmesan cheese would add 1.1 gram of fat to each serving.

on the liteside

baked salmon

on the liteside

4   salmon steaks, desired size
         juice of $1/_2$ lemon
1   medium onion, minced
1   large stalk celery, chopped
1   Tbsp. water or cooking wine
         Butter Flavor Granules* or butter flavor cooking spray

Sprinkle lemon juice on steaks and set aside. Prepare onions and celery and put in bottom of baking dish. Pour water or wine into dish and lay fish on top onions and celery. Sprinkle top of fish with butter flavor granules, or lightly spray with butter flavor cooking spray. Cover with foil and bake in preheated 400 degree oven for 20 minutes or until fish is done and flakes easily.

*Butter Buds and Molly McButter are two brands which are very good.

baked chicken breasts serves 4

olive oil cooking spray
4   boneless, skinless chicken breasts
1   medium red pepper, sliced thin
1   medium yellow or green pepper, sliced thin
1   large onion, sliced into rings
2   large tomatoes, peeled, seeded, and chopped
1   cup fresh basil, chopped (can substitute 1 Tbsp. dried basil)

Spray non-stick skillet with cooking spray and over medium heat, brown chicken. Remove to baking dish and set aside. Spray skillet once again and sauté the peppers and onions for several minutes. Add the tomatoes and basil to skillet, mixing well. Pour this mixture over the browned chicken breasts, cover with foil and bake 30 minutes in a preheated 400 degree oven. Serve with rice.

on the liteside

lemon cheesecake serves 10

	vegetable cooking spray
$1/_4$	cup graham cracker crumbs
2	16 oz. packages fat free cream cheese
1	14 oz. can fat free or low fat sweetened condensed milk
4	egg whites
1	whole egg
$1/_3$	cup fresh lemon juice
1	tsp. vanilla extract
$1/_2$	tsp. lemon extract
$1/_3$	cup unsifted flour
1	cup fresh strawberries

Spray bottom of 8 inch springform pan with cooking spray; sprinkle crumbs evenly in bottom of pan. Beat cream cheese until fluffy; slowly add sweetened condensed milk and continue to beat until smooth. Add egg whites, egg, lemon juice, vanilla, and lemon extract; mix well. Add flour, stir until mixed well, and pour into prepared pan. Bake 50 to 55 minutes or until center is set. Cool, chill, and serve with strawberries. Keep cheesecake refrigerated.

breads

breads

Alabama biscuits yields 15

2½   cups flour
2   tsp. baking powder
2   Tbsp. sugar
½   tsp. salt
1   package dry yeast
¼   cup warm water
2   Tbsp. Crisco Oil
¾   cup warm milk

Sift together flour, baking powder, sugar and salt.

Dissolve dry yeast in ¼ cup warm water. Combine 2 Tbsp. Crisco Oil and ¾ cup warm milk, add milk mixture along with the yeast to dry ingredients. Mix well, either with dough hook or by hand. If by hand, knead about 5-7 minutes.

Roll out about ¼ in. thick on floured board surface. Cut with a small biscuit cutter. Dip in melted butter and stack one on top of the other, forming one biscuit. Let rise for 1 hour and bake at 425 degees until brown. Use a large cutter or glass to make a hamburger bun. Serve immediately

We don't know why they're called Alabama Biscuits but one thing for sure, they are so g-o-o-d! Alabamas are a special request and usually a standard item at any family dinner. Even those who constantly say they are dieting have several (usually with butter and homemade preserves).

 source: Bertha Craft Mays

buttermilk biscuits yields 15 biscuits

2	cups of flour	1	heaping Tbsp. baking powder
1	tsp. salt	$^2/_3$	cup shortening
1	Tbsp. sugar	1	cup buttermilk

Thoroughly mix all ingredients into a soft dough. Roll out on a floured surface about 1/3 inch to 1/2 inch thick. Cut with standard size biscuit cutter. Bake at 475 degrees for 15 minutes. Do not overmix. Too much handling will cause biscuits to be tough.

yeast biscuits yields 3 dozen

$2^1/_2$	cups all purpose flour	$^1/_2$	tsp. soda
$^1/_2$	tsp. salt	1	cup buttermilk
1	Tbsp. sugar	$^1/_2$	cake yeast
3	Tbsp. shortening	3	Tbsp. water

Mix together flour, salt, and sugar; cut shortening in with pastry cutter. Add soda to buttermilk. Dissolve yeast in water, add buttermilk; stir into flour mixture, mixing well.

Place on floured board and knead dough lightly. Roll out to $^1/_4$ inch and cut with biscuit cutter or small glass. Place on ungreased baking sheet and bake in preheated 400 degree oven 10 to 15 minutes or until golden brown. Ovens may vary.

breads

skillet corn bread

2   Tbsp. butter
$^3/_4$ cup corn meal
1   cup flour
2   Tbsp. sugar
$^1/_2$ tsp. salt
3   tsp. baking powder
2   eggs, well beaten
$^2/_3$ cup milk

Preheat oven to 450 degrees. Put butter in 10 inch iron skillet and place in oven to melt.

Sift dry ingredients together; add eggs and milk and mix well. Make sure that skillet is very hot and butter has melted; pour butter into cornbread mixture and the mixture back into the skillet.

Bake 15 minutes or until golden brown.

Great with pinto beans, and cucumbers and onions. (see recipes).

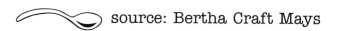 source: Bertha Craft Mays

spoon bread soufflé serves 6

3	cups milk
$^3/_4$	cups yellow corn meal
5	egg yolks, well beaten (reserve whites)
$1^1/_2$	tsp. salt
3	Tbsp. sugar
5	Tbsp. melted butter
$1^1/_2$	tsp. baking powder

In 3 qt. heavy saucepan, heat milk until hot; stir in cornmeal. Heat, stirring constantly until thin mush consistency. Remove from heat.

Mix together beaten yolks, salt, sugar, butter, and baking powder. Stir into corn meal mixture. Beat egg whites until stiff and fold into corn meal mixture.

Pour into greased 10 inch or 2 qt. baking dish and bake in preheated 350 degree oven for 45 minutes or until golden brown. Serve immediately.

Margarine and skim milk may be used in place of butter and whole milk.

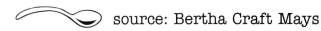 source: Bertha Craft Mays

spoon bread serves 10

1	qt. milk
1	stick margarine or butter
1	cup yellow corn meal
4	eggs
$1\frac{1}{2}$	Tbsp. sugar
1	Tbsp. baking powder
$\frac{3}{4}$	tsp. salt

In large saucepan, heat milk and butter until hot. Add corn meal, beat with wire whip or beater until thoroughly mixed. Let cool slightly. The cornmeal mixture will be thickened. Beat eggs; add sugar, baking powder, and salt. Add egg mixture to cooled cornmeal mixture. Stir well to mix. Pour into greased or sprayed baking dish and bake at 350 degrees for 30 to 40 minutes or until golden brown. Serve hot with butter.

Can be made ahead and refrigerated for up to 6 hours before baking. (Baking time will vary because mixture will be cold.) Any left over can be refrigerated and reheated in microwave until piping hot. The consistency of the reheated spoon bread will be drier but still good.

breads

homemade french toast makes 4 slices

2	eggs, well beaten
$1/_2$	cup milk
1	tsp. sugar
1	tsp. cinnamon
$1/_4$	tsp. vanilla
4	slices day-old homemade bread, 1 inch thick

Mix all ingredients to make egg batter. Dip bread into batter, thoroughly coating both sides. Fry in small amount of fat on griddle until golden brown and crisp.

Serve with butter and maple syrup. Also great with Mrs. Rowe's Old Fashioned Recipe Preserves.

breads

pecan french toast   serves 6

breads

4	large eggs, lightly beaten
$1/4$	cup sugar
1	cup milk
$1/2$	tsp. vanilla extract
1	16 oz. loaf french, italian or homemade bread cut into 1 in. slices
$2/3$	cup butter or margarine, melted
$1/2$	cup pecans, chopped

Combinee first four ingredients, stirring well. Place bread slices in a single layer into lightly greased baking dish. Pour egg mixture over bread slices; cover and refrigerator overnight, turning bread once.

Pour butter into a jelly roll pan; place bread slices in a single layer in pan.

Bake in preheated oven at 400 degrees for 10 minutes. Sprinkle with pecans. Return to oven and bake an additional 10 to 15 minutes. Serve immediately with maple syrup.

banana nut bread

$^1/_2$	cup pecans
$^1/_2$	cup raisins
$1^1/_2$	cups flour
$^3/_4$	tsp. soda
1	stick butter or margarine, softened
1	cup sugar
2	eggs
3	medium ripe bananas, mashed

Grease and flour a 9x5x3 inch loaf pan and set aside. Preheat oven at 350 degrees. Dust nuts and raisins with small amount of flour and combine remaining flour with soda. Set aside.

Cream butter and sugar together. Add eggs one at a time and beat well. Add flour a little at a time, mixing well after each addition. Stir in bananas, nuts and raisins. Pour in prepared loaf pan and bake for 50 minutes or till done. Cool on rack for ten minutes, remove from pan and continue to cool on rack. When completely cool, wrap in foil and keep a day or two before eating. This allows the bread to become more moist.

breads

buttermilk rolls   yield 2 dozen

$^3/_4$ cup warm water
$^1/_4$ cup sugar
2   packages dry yeast
2   eggs, beaten
$1^1/_2$ cups warm buttermilk
2   Tbsp. Crisco Oil
1   tsp. salt
5-6   cups flour
        melted butter

Mix together warm water, sugar and yeast. Set aside.

Beat eggs in large bowl. Add buttermilk, oil and salt to beaten eggs.

Add yeast mixture to egg-milk batter. Mix. Stir 5 cups of flour into batter and mix. (May have to add up to 6 cups for proper consistency.) When mixed, put on floured surface and knead well (10 to 15 minutes). Cover and let rise until doubled in size.

Shape into small rolls, place in greased pan or on baking sheet, and let rise 45 minutes to 1 hour. Bake in preheated 400 degree oven 12 minutes or until brown. Remove from oven and brush with melted butter. Serve immediately.

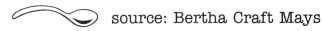 source: Bertha Craft Mays

breads

Yorkshire pudding 6 to 8 servings

$1/_2$ cup melted fat or beef drippings
1   cup flour
$1/_2$ tsp. salt
1   cup milk
2   eggs

Preheat oven to 450 degrees. Pour fat or drippings into an 8 inch iron skillet or square pan and heat in the oven until sizzling hot.

Mix flour and salt in large bowl; combine milk and eggs and add to flour. Beat with electric mixer until smooth. Remove sizzling pan from oven, pour mixture in quickly and return to oven. Bake for 30 minutes or until pudding has risen well and is brown and crisp. The center may fall which is characteristic of Yorkshire pudding.

Cut pudding into serving squares and serve on platter with roast beef.

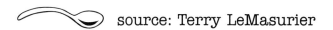 source: Terry LeMasurier

Terry, who is from Essex, England, shared his Mum's favorite Yorkshire pudding recipe.

breads

buttermilk pancakes

1	cup buttermilk
1	cup flour
1	beaten egg
1	tsp. baking powder
1	tsp. sugar
1	tsp. soda
$^1/_2$	tsp. salt

Have buttermilk stand at room temperature 12 hours before mixing. Mix all ingredients together and cook on hot greased griddle.

Good variation is to grate fresh apples, mix with cinnamon and pour into batter.

pancake batter

$1^3/_4$ cups all purpose flour
4   tsp. sugar
3   tsp. baking powder
$^1/_2$ tsp. salt
$1^1/_2$ cups milk
2   beaten eggs
2   Tbsp. liquid shortening, do not use butter

Sift together flour, sugar, baking powder and salt. Add milk and eggs. Beat on low speed until mixed and smooth. Add liquid shortening; blend until smooth. Place in tight container and refrigerate. Leave overnight before using. If tightly covered will keep one week.

Good with warm Highland County Maple Syrup and chopped pecans.

pumpkin pecan pancakes   serve 4

2	cups all-purpose flour
4	tsp. baking powder
1	tsp. ground cinnamon
$^1/_2$	tsp. ground nutmeg
$^1/_4$	tsp. ground allspice
$^3/_4$	cup sugar
$1^1/_2$	cups solid pack pumpkin
3	eggs
1	cup milk
$^3/_4$	cup vegetable oil (Crisco preferred)
1	tsp. vanilla extract
4	oz. chopped pecans

Sift dry ingredients and set aside. Using a large bowl, combine pumpkin, eggs, milk, oil, and vanilla. Add dry ingredients and stir until blended; stir in pecans just before ready to cook.

A hot greased griddle is best for cooking pancakes. Pour $^1/_4$ cup batter onto griddle and cook until bubbles form and bottom is brown. Turn and brown the other side. Serve with warm pure Maple syrup.

If preferred, omit the pecans from the batter and add to the syrup. Heat and pour oven pancakes.

cakes & frostings

cakes &
frostings

cakes, continued

frostings

fillings

cakes &
frostings

fresh apple pound cake

2   cups sugar
$1^1/_2$ cups cooking oil
4   eggs
$^3/_4$ tsp. salt
1   tsp. soda
3   cups flour
3   cups diced apples
1   cup chopped pecans
1   cup coconut
1   tsp. vanilla

Mix sugar and oil. Add eggs one at a time and beat after each. Sift together salt, soda and flour. Add to egg mixture and beat well. Add apples, nuts, coconut and vanilla. Bake in greased and floured tube pan. Do not open door while cake is baking. Bake for 1 hour 20 minutes at 325 degrees. If using loaf pans, fill $^2/_3$ full and bake 40-45 minutes.

Family favorite.

topping
$1^1/_2$ cups brown sugar
1   stick butter
$^1/_2$ cup chopped nuts
3   tsp. milk

Place all ingredients in saucepan and bring to boil. Cook until soft ball stage. Pour on cake while warm.

cakes & frostings

best ever pound cake

3	sticks butter, softened
$^1/_2$	cup Crisco
3	cups sugar
6	eggs
4	cups flour
1	cup milk
1	tsp. vanilla extract
1	tsp. lemon extract

Grease and coat with flour a 10 inch tube pan (see cake baking tips). Set aside.

Cream butter and Crisco at medium speed with an electric mixer about 2 minutes or until soft and creamy. This step whips air into the cake, so it will rise during baking. Gradually add sugar, beating at medium speed 5 to 7 minutes or until mixture reaches a fluffy consistency.

Add eggs, one at a time, beating just until yellow disappears. Overmixing causes a tough crust and heavy texture.

Gradually add one-fourth flour alternately with one-third milk, beating at lowest speed with mixer and begining and ending with flour. Mix just until blended after each addition. Scrape bottom and sides of bowl several times with a rubber spatula to uniformly mix batter. Stir in extracts.

cakes & frostings

Spoon batter evenly into prepared cake pan; smooth top and place pan in center of preheated 325 degree oven. Temperature too low causes the cake to fall. If the cake is placed on a rack too low in oven, the bottom of the cake will become too brown. Bake for $1\frac{1}{2}$ hours. Test for doneness with a cake tester or wooden pick. Insert in the center of the cake; it should come out clean. Underbaking results in a damp cake and sinking in the center.

Cool the cake in pan on a wire rack for 15 minutes. Run a knife around sides to completely loosen and invert onto a wire rack. Cake should easily slip out; invert onto another wire rack so that the rounded top is up and flat crusty bottom is down. Let cool completely.

Store in an airtight container or wrap with plastic wrap and aluminum foil and freeze up to two months. Thaw without unwrapping.

Family favorite.

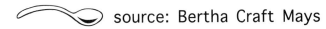 source: Bertha Craft Mays

cakes & frostings

chocolate pound cake

$1/2$	cup Crisco		$1/2$	tsp. salt
2	sticks butter		4	Tbsp. cocoa
3	cups sugar		1	cup milk
5	eggs		1	Tbsp. vanilla
3	cups flour			
$1/2$	tsp. baking powder			

Cream shortening and butter well. Add sugar. Mix well. Add eggs one at a time. Sift dry ingredients together, adding alternately with milk and vanilla.

Pour into greased, floured tube pan. Bake in preheated 325 degree oven for 1 hour 20 minutes and test.

chocolate icing

$1/4$	cup and 2 squares unsweetened chocolate
1	lb. powdered sugar
1	tsp. vanilla

Melt unsweetened chocolate. Stir in powdered sugar and vanilla. Mix well

 source: Linda Hanna

german chocolate pound cake

1	4 oz. package sweet german chocolate
2	cups sugar
$1/2$	cup butter
$1/2$	cup shortening
4	eggs, beaten
2	tsp. pure vanilla
1	cup buttermilk
3	cups sifted all-purpose flour
$1/2$	tsp. soda
1	tsp. salt
	powdered sugar

Grease and dust with flour a 9 inch tube pan. Preheat oven to 300 degrees.

Soften chocolate in double boiler; set aside. With electric beaters cream sugar, butter, and shortening. Mix in eggs, vanilla and buttermilk until blended. Sift together flour, soda, and salt; add to creamed mixture and mix well. Stir in chocolate and blend.

Spoon into prepared cake pan and bake $1^1/2$ hours. Test with tester or wooden pick for doneness. Tester should come out clean. Invert on cake plate to cool and do not remove cake pan. After about 25 minutes, remove pan and continue to cool completely. Dust with powdered sugar.

cakes & frostings

fresh apple cake with caramel sauce

$1^1/_2$ cups Crisco oil*
2 cups sugar
2 eggs
2 cups flour
1 tsp. soda
1 tsp. cinnamon

2 tsp. vanilla
3 cups apples, peeled,
    chopped or shredded
1 cup coconut
1 cup nuts
1 cup raisins

*Crisco oil is recommended because it is very light and if heavy oil is used the cake will taste oily. If Crisco oil is not used, reduce oil to $1^1/_4$ cups.

Mix together oil, sugar, and eggs. Sift together flour, soda, and cinnamon; stir into oil mixture. Add remaining ingredients and pour into greased floured 13x9x2 inch cake pan.

Bake at 350 degrees for 50 minutes. Test for doneness with cake tester or wooden pick. Pour glaze over cake while it is hot. Cool on wire rack and cut into squares. Serve with vanilla ice cream and warm caramel sauce.

glaze
$^1/_2$ stick butter or margarine, melted
1 oz. milk
$^1/_2$ cup plus 1 Tbsp. powdered sugar

Stir together and bring to a boil. Pour over cake while hot.

 source: Pearl Craft McCaleb

cakes & frostings

warm caramel sauce

1   cup sugar
$^1/_2$ cup water
$^3/_4$ cup whipping cream
1   Tbsp. butter

In a heavy saucepan over medium-high heat, combine sugar and water. Boil for 15 minutes without stirring, until syrup turns to amber. Do not overcook. Remove from heat and cool 2 to 3 minutes.

Pour in cream and stir in butter. Resume cooking, stirring constantly, until smooth. Serve warm over cake.

Sauce can be refrigerated and reheated over low heat or in microwave before serving.

If you choose not to make your sauce, there are commercial sauces available which are very good. One in particular is Smuckers Special Recipe Butterscotch Caramel Topping which is delicious!

Other serving suggestions:

Serve warm with vanilla custard sauce, rum custard sauce or lemon sauce.

cakes & frostings

Grandma Ruth Finley's applesauce cake

1	lb. raisins	1	Tbsp. nutmeg
1	lb. nuts	2	tsp. soda
4	cups flour	2	cups butter
1	Tbsp. cloves	2	cups sugar
1	tsp. baking powder	4	eggs
1	Tbsp. cinnamon	3	cups applesauce
			10X powdered sugar

Grease and flour a 10-inch tube pan. Preheat oven 300 degrees. Dust raisins and nuts with a very small amount of flour. (This prevents them from sinking to the bottom of the cake.) Sift together remaining flour, cloves, baking powder, cinnamon, nutmeg, and soda; set aside.

Cream butter and sugar until smooth and creamy. Add eggs one at a time and blend only until the yellow has disappeared. Add dry ingredients alternately with applesauce, blending until mixed. Stir in raisins and nuts.

Spoon into prepared tube pan and bake for 2 hours. Test for doneness with a cake tester or wooden pick. Cool in pan or on wire rack for 15 minutes. Remove from pan and cool, completely on wire rack. Turn right side up and dust with powdered sugar.

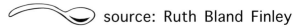 source: Ruth Bland Finley

Grandma Finely never used an electric mixer. She made all of her cakes by mixing with a large wooden spoon and they were delicious!

cakes & frostings

1-2-3-4 cake

1	cup butter	3	tsp. baking powder
2	cups sugar	$1/2$	tsp. salt
4	eggs	1	cup milk
3	cups flour	1	tsp. vanilla

Cream butter until fluffy. Add sugar and cream well. Add eggs one at a time. Beat well. Sift flour, baking powder and salt together. Add alternating with milk ending with flour. Beat on low speed. Add vanilla.

Pour into greased, floured pans. Makes three layers. Bake at 350 degrees for 30 minutes. Test for doneness.

7 minute icing

2	egg whites	1	Tbsp. white Karo Syrup
$1^{1}/2$	cups sugar	$1/4$	tsp. cream of tartar
5	Tbsp. water		

Combine all ingredients. Cook in double boiler approximately 7 minutes, beating constantly while icing cooks.

quick & easy coconut layer cake

1	box white or yellow cake mix
8	oz. sour cream
1	8 oz. pkg. frozen coconut, thawed
$1^1/_2$	cups sugar
12	oz. container of cool whip

Several days before serving, mix cake according to box instructions. Cool completely; wrap with stretch wrap or aluminum foil and refrigerate or freeze until layers are firm. Cut each layer horizontally making 4 layers. Prepare filling by combining sour cream, $^3/_4$ package of coconut, and sugar together; Mix well and spread between each layer.

Frost cake completely with cool whip and sprinkle remaining coconut on top. Place in sealed container in refrigerator for several days before serving.

Even though this is not a "made from scratch" cake, it is delicious!

cakes & frostings

lemon-filled coconut cake

This cake may be made from scratch (see 1-2-3-4 cake recipe) or the quick and easy way. The quick method uses 1 box of 2 layer white cake mix, made according to instructions.

lemon filling

$1^1/_4$	cup sugar		3	Tbsp. lemon juice
$^1/_4$	cup cornstarch		1	grated lemon rind
1	cup plus 2 Tbsp. boiling water		2	Tbsp. butter
4	egg yolks, lightly beaten			

Combine sugar and cornstarch in medium saucepan; stir in water. Cook over medium heat, stirring constantly, until sugar and cornstarch dissolve. Gradually stir about one fourth of hot mixture into yolks; return this mixture to remaining hot mixture, stirring constantly with a wire whisk. Stir in lemon juice and rind.

Cook, stirring constantly, until mixture is thickened. Remove from heat; stir in butter, and let cool, stirring occasionally. When completely cooled, spread between layers of cake.

icing

Can use 7 minute icing (see recipe)
The quick method uses a 12 oz. non-dairy whipped topping, such as Cool Whip, mixed with $^3/_4$ cup coconut to ice the top and sides. Sprinkle about $^1/_4$ cup coconut on outside of cake.

Refrigerate several hours before cutting and refrigerate any leftover cake.

cakes & frostings

eight layer cake

1$^1/_2$	cups butter	4$^1/_2$	tsp. baking powder
3	cups sugar	1	tsp. salt
6	large eggs	1$^1/_2$	cup milk
4$^1/_2$	cups flour	2	tsp. vanilla

Cream butter until fluffy. Add sugar and cream well. Add eggs one at a time, beat well. Sift flour, baking powder and salt together; add alternating with milk, ending with flour. Beat on low speed, add vanilla. Pour $^1/_2$ cup of batter into greased, floured 9$^1/_2$ inch cake pans. The batter will barely cover the bottom to produce a thin layer when baked. Bake in a 350 degree oven for 10 to 15 minutes. Test for doneness. Makes 8 or 9 layers. Cool in pan on rack 10 minutes, then turn out on towel to finish cooling. Cool completely before icing the cake.

chocolate icing

2	sticks margarine
$^3/_4$	cup milk
8	Tbsp. cocoa
2	boxes 10X sugar
2	tsp. vanilla

Bring first 3 ingredients to a boil. Add sugar and vanilla. Beat well. If icing is too stiff, add a little milk and mix well.

This cake is made for those who love the icing more than the cake.

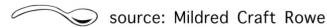 source: Mildred Craft Rowe

cakes & frostings

butterscotch icing

1 cup brown sugar, firmly packed
3 Tbsp. solid shortening (Crisco)
2 Tbsp. butter
$1/4$ tsp. salt
$1/4$ cup milk
$1\frac{1}{2}$ cups sifted confectioner's sugar

Combine sugar, shortening, butter, and salt in saucepan and bring to boil, stirring constantly. Add milk and cook over low heat for 3 minutes. Cool; add confectioner's sugar and beat until thick enough to spread.

peanut butter icing

$1/4$ cup peanut butter
2 Tbsp. margarine
$2\frac{1}{2}$ cups 10X sugar
$1/4$ cup milk
$1/2$ tsp. vanilla

Cream peanut butter and margarine together. Add sugar slowly, then milk and vanilla. Stir until smooth. *Great on brownies!*

seafoam icing

2 cups sugar
$1/4$ tsp. cream of tartar
$2/3$ cup water
1 tsp. vanilla
3 egg whites

Mix sugar, cream of tartar, and water. Cook until it will spin a good thread. Add vanilla. Beat egg whites and pour syrup into them, beating until firm.
Especially good on Devil's Food or Brown Stone Front Cake.

cakes & frostings

Aunt Sissy's chocolate cake

$1/_2$	cup butter	2	cups cake flour
2	cups sugar	2	tsp. baking powder
2	eggs	$1^1/_2$	cups milk
4	squares melted chocolate, cooled	2	tsp. vanilla

Cream together butter and sugar. Add eggs, one at a time, and chocolate. Sift together flour and baking powder and add to butter mixture alternately with milk. Add vanilla.

Pour into 2 well greased and floured 9 inch pans. Bake in preheated 350 degree oven for 25 minutes.

Aunt Sissy's chocolate icing

$1/_2$	cup butter	1	egg, beaten
2	squares unsweetened chocolate		pinch of salt
$1^1/_2$	cup confectioners sugar	1	tsp. vanilla

Melt butter and chocolate in double boiler. Remove from heat. Blend sugar, egg, salt and vanilla into chocolate mixture. Beat until icing is creamy. Double for 3 layers.

By mistake, I used semi-sweet chocolate which made a very sweet icing but good enough to eat with a spoon.

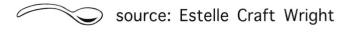 source: Estelle Craft Wright

brown stone front cake

$3/_4$	cup cocoa	3	cups white sugar
2	tsp. soda	4	eggs
1	cup boiling water	4	cups flour, sifted
1	cup butter	1	cup buttermilk

Grease and flour 10 inch cake pans. Preheat oven to 350 degrees. Mix together cocoa and soda; pour boiling water over mixture and set aside.

Cream butter until creamy and smooth, add sugar and continue to blend. Add eggs one at a time, blending well after each addition. Add flour alternately with buttermilk and continue to mix. Just prior to baking, add cocoa-soda mixture.

Divide batter evenly into pans and bake 12 to 15 minutes. Test for doneness. Cool on wire rack; cool completely before icing. Spread caramel icing between layers and over top and sides.

See two recipes for caramel icing on next page

cakes & frostings

caramel icing I

1   lb. brown sugar
1   cup cream
      piece of butter size of
         a walnut (about 1 Tbsp.)

Boil sugar and cream until it reaches the soft ball stage when dropped in cold water. Add butter just before removing from the heat. Set aside to cool. Beat until smooth and creamy. Ice cake.

caramel icing II

$1^1/_2$ cups dark brown sugar
$^1/_2$ cup white sugar
$^1/_2$ cup milk
$^1/_2$ stick butter
1   tsp. vanilla
$^1/_2$ cup confectioners sugar
2   Tbsp. milk

Cook brown sugar, white sugar and 1/2 cup milk until mixture forms a soft ball in cold water. Add butter and vanilla. Beat until it starts to get firm, add confectioners sugar and 2 Tbsp. of milk. Stir to mix. Let cool and ice cake.

cakes & frostings

carrot cake with cream cheese icing

2	cups sugar	2	tsp. soda
2	tsp. cinnamon	1$\frac{1}{2}$	cups vegetable oil
2	cups flour	4	eggs
1	tsp. salt	3	cups grated carrots

Grease and flour three 9 inch cake pans. Preheat oven to 350 degrees.

Sift dry ingredients in a large bowl; add oil and blend. Add eggs one at a time, beat after each addition. Blend in carrots.

Pour into prepared pans. Bake for 30 minutes or until done. Remove to wire rack to cool slightly. Invert onto cake plate and ice cake while still warm.

Makes a large rich cake. Excellent!

cream cheese icing

8	oz. cream cheese
1	stick margarine, room temperature
1	lb. box 10X powdered sugar
1	tsp. vanilla
1	cup chopped pecans

Cream the cream cheese and margarine together. Add powdered sugar and mix well. Add remaining ingredients. Ice cake while still warm.

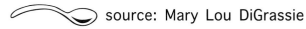 source: Mary Lou DiGrassie

cakes & frostings

graham cracker cake with pineapple filling

1	cup milk
16	oz. graham cracker crumbs
2	cups sugar
2	sticks butter, room temperature
4	eggs
1	cup coconut
1	tsp. vanilla
1	tsp. baking powder
1	cup chopped nuts

Preheat oven to 350 degrees. Grease and flour three 9 inch round cake pans.

In large mixing bowl, pour milk over graham cracker crumbs. Cream sugar and butter; add eggs one at a time, blending well after each addition. Add to milk-crumb mixture and mix well. Stir in coconut, vanilla, baking powder and nuts.

Pour into prepared pans and bake for 25 minutes or until done. Cool on wire rack and spread filling between layers and on top.

pineapple filling

1	lb. box 10X powdered sugar
$1/2$	stick butter, room temperature
1	cup drained crushed pineapple

Mix ingredients well.

pineapple upside-down cake

1	stick butter
1	cup brown sugar
1	medium can pineapple rings (save juices) 7 slices
7	maraschino cherries
$1/4$	cup chopped pecans
3	eggs, separated
9	Tbsp. pineapple juice
1	cup sugar
1	cup flour
3	tsp. baking powder
1	tsp. vanilla

prepare pan

Melt butter in heavy cast iron skillet. Spread the brown sugar evenly. Lay on pineapple rings and place cherries in the center of the rings. Sprinkle pecans on top.

batter

Beat egg yolks; add sugar and juice and mix together. Sift flour and baking powder together and stir into mixture. Add vanilla, beat egg whites and fold into batter. Pour into skillet and bake at 350 degrees for 30 minutes. Remove from oven and invert on a cake plate.

Excellent served warm with slightly sweetened whipped cream.

cakes & frostings

easy pineapple upside-down cake

1	stick butter or margarine, melted
1	cup brown sugar
1	medium can pineapple (7 slices)
7	maraschino cherries
$1/4$	cup chopped pecans
1	box yellow cake mix (1 layer size)

Pour melted butter into a 9 inch square pan. Spread sugar evenly over top; lay pineapple rings on top and place a cherry in center of each ring. Sprinkle pecans over pineapple.

Prepare cake mix according to directions on box. Pour into prepared pan and bake in preheated oven at 350 degrees for 30 minutes or browned.

cakes & frostings

pies

pies

pies, continued

pies

cheese and cream apple pie

	pastry for 9 inch shell
1	Tbsp. flour
1	Tbsp. sugar
5	cups diced apples
1	cup sugar
$^1/_2$	tsp. nutmeg
8	slices American cheese, diced
1	cup half and half cream

Line pie pan with pastry, mix together 1 Tbsp. flour and 1 Tbsp. sugar and sprinkle over bottom. Toss together apples, sugar, nutmeg and diced cheese. Place in a pastry lined pan. Pour cream over the filling. Cover with a lattice pastry top and bake at 375 degrees for 30 to 35 minutes or until well done and lightly browned.

This is by far the best apple pie I've ever tasted. I first tasted this pie twenty-five years ago. I begged Mother to make it again and again. Finally after much nagging, she confessed that she'd lost her recipe. There is a happy ending. While preparing for this cookbook, Mother went through all her shoe boxes to sort recipes and Glory be! She found my favorite apple pie recipe.

- Ginger LeMasuier

pies

apple pie

1	cup sugar
2	Tbsp. flour
	dash salt
1	tsp. cinnamon
1	tsp. nutmeg
1	Tbsp. lemon juice
7	tart apples, peeled, cored, and sliced
1	tsp. sugar
$^1/_4$	stick butter or margarine, thinly sliced
	Pie dough, enough for a double deep dish 9 inch crust
	melted butter

Preheat oven to 450 degrees and prepare dough for pie crust.

Combine all dry ingredients; sprinkle apple slices with lemon juice and gently toss with dry ingredients. Line pie pan with bottom crust, leaving about an inch overhang and fill with apples slices; dot with butter. Cover with top crust, crimp the edges, and trim any excess. Cut six 2-inch slits evenly around the top of the pie for steam to escape and to test apples for doneness after baking. Sprinkle sugar over top. To prevent edges from overbrowning, gently fold a strip of foil around rim of crust, covering the fluted edge. Remove in last 10 minutes of baking.

Reduce oven temperature to 350 degrees and bake for 55 to 60 minutes or until apples are done and crust is golden brown. Brush with butter and cool on a pie rack. Serve with nutmeg sauce or cinnamon ice cream.

Use tart and firm apples like Granny Smith, Pippin, Stayman, Rambo, and York. May use 2 (#2) cans drained sliced pie apples if fresh apples are not available.

pies

nutmeg sauce

1	cup sugar
1	Tbsp. flour
	pinch salt
2	cups boiling water
1	Tbsp. butter
1	tsp. nutmeg

Mix well the sugar, flour and salt; add boiling water gradually, stirring constantly. Add butter and cook for five minutes. Remove from heat and stir in nutmeg; serve hot.

brown sugar walnut topping

$^2/_3$	cup brown sugar
$^1/_2$	cup walnuts
3	tsp. melted butter

Mix together ingredients. Sprinkle on top of pumpkin pie, place under broiler. Broil until sugar is bubbly.

pies

B.B.'s fried apple butter pies makes 8 pies

2	cups all purpose flour
1	tsp. salt
$^2/_3$	cup Crisco or other solid shortening
$^1/_2$	stick butter
	milk
2	cups apple butter
	shortening and butter for frying

Mix flour, salt, shortening, and butter together with fork or pastry blender until consistency of cornmeal. Add just enough milk to moisten and mix. Divide into 8 balls of dough; roll out each into a round pastry. Fill each pastry with 2 Tbsp. of apple butter; fold over and seal edges by pressing with fork. Fry in equal amounts of shortening and butter, amounts determined by the size of the frying pan used.

These are best with homemade spicy apple butter

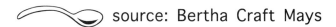 source: Bertha Craft Mays

pies

original coconut cream pie

3	egg yolks (reserve whites for meringue)
1	cup sugar
4	Tbsp. cornstarch
	cold water
3	cups milk
1	cup coconut
2	tsp. vanilla
1	Tbsp. butter
1	baked 9 inch deep pie crust

Mix yolks, sugar, and cornstarch together with enough cold water to make a paste. Using a double boiler, heat milk to boiling. Add egg mixture, stir occasionally, and cook about 4 minutes, until very thick. Remove from heat and stir in $3/4$ cup coconut,butter and vanilla.

Pour into a baked 9 inch deep dish crust, top with meringue and sprinkle with remaining coconut. Bake in preheated 325 degree oven until golden brown, about 30 minutes. Cool on wire rack.

pies

chocolate meringue pie

3	egg yolks
1	cup sugar
4	heaping Tbsp. cocoa
4	Tbsp. cornstarch
	cold water
3	cups milk
1	Tbsp. butter
2	tsp. vanilla
1	baked 9 inch deep dish pie crust

Mix yolks, sugar, cocoa, and cornstarch together with enough water to make a paste. Using a double boiler, heat milk to boiling; add egg mixture, stir occasionally and cook until very thick, about 4 minutes. Remove from heat and stir in butter and vanilla.

Pour into pie crust; top with meringue and bake in preheated 325 degree oven until golden brown, about 30 minutes. Cool on wire rack.

pies

butterscotch pie

3	egg yolks
1	cup firmly packed brown sugar
4	Tbsp. cornstarch
	cold water
3	cups milk
1	Tbsp butter
2	tsp. vanilla
1	baked 9 inch deep dish pie crust

Mix yolks, sugar, and cornstarch together with enough water to make a paste. Using a double boiler, heat milk to boiling; add egg mixture, stir occasionally, and cook until thick, about 4 minutes. Remove from heat and stir in butter and vanilla.

Pour into crust, top with meringue and bake in preheated 325 degree oven for 30 minutes or until golden brown. Cool on wire rack.

old fashioned egg custard pie

makes 10$^{1}/_{2}$ inch pie

1	cup sugar
5	eggs
	dash of nutmeg
2	tsp. vanilla
4	cups milk

Beat together sugar, eggs, nutmeg and vanilla. Then add milk. Mix together and pour into unbaked pie shell. Sprinkle top with nutmeg. Bake at 350 degrees for 45 minutes or until set.

lemon chess pie

$^{1}/_{2}$	stick butter, melted
1$^{1}/_{2}$	cups sugar
3	eggs, beaten
1	Tbsp. cornmeal
	juice of 1$^{1}/_{2}$ lemons
1	unbaked 9 inch shell

Melt butter and add sugar; add beaten eggs and cornmeal. Mix together and add lemon juice last. Pour into pie shell and bake in preheated 350 degree oven for 35 to 45 minutes.

pies

never fail lemon pie

$1/2$	cup fresh lemon juice, strained
$1/4$	tsp. lemon extract
1	15 oz. can sweetened condensed milk*
2	egg yolks
1	9 inch baked pie crust
$1/4$	tsp. cream of tartar
2	egg whites
4	Tbsp. sugar

Combine lemon juice and extract and using an electric mixer on low speed, slowly blend with milk. Add yolks and stir until well blended; pour into pie crust. Add cream of tartar to egg whites. Beat until almost stiff enough to hold peak. Add sugar gradually, beating until stiff but not dry. Pile lightly on pie, seal edges to prevent weeping, and bake in 325 degree oven until lightly browned, about 15 to 20 minutes. Cool on wire rack. *can substitute low fat or fat free sweetened condensed milk. Very tart and rich. To add a little zip, substitute Gingersnap Pie Crust.

gingersnap pie crust

10	finely crushed gingersnaps
4	finely crushed graham crackers*
$1/4$	cup butter, melted
2	Tbsp. sugar

Thoroughly mix all ingredients; press the mixture evenly in a 9 inch pie pan. Bake in preheated 375 degree oven for 4 to 5 minutes.   *count whole rectangle cracker as one cracker.

pies

lemon meringue pie

3	Tbsp. cold water
3	Tbsp. cornstarch
2	Tbsp flour
$2\frac{1}{4}$	cups hot water
$1\frac{3}{4}$	cups plus 3 Tbsp. sugar
3	egg yolks, lightly beaten
$1\frac{1}{2}$	lemon (grated rind and juice)
1	Tbsp. butter
1	baked 9 inch crust

Mix the cornstarch and flour and add enough cold water to make a thin paste. Combine hot water and sugar in top of double boiler and bring to boil over direct heat. Add cornstarch paste and, stirring constantly, cook until mixture begins to thicken. Return to double boiler and cook until thick and smooth (about 15 minutes)

Stir in small amount of thickened mixture into beaten egg yolks to blend; return yolks to hot mixture and cook a few minutes longer. Stir in lemon rind, juice, and butter. Cool, stirring occasionally. Pour into baked crust. Top with meringue. (see meringue recipe.)

pies

mudd pie

$1^1/_2$ cups Chocolate Wafers, crumbled
3   Tbsp. margarine
1   cup chocolate semi-sweet bits
$^2/_3$ cup marshmallows
1   ($5^3/_4$ oz.) can evaporated milk
1   qt. coffee ice cream
$^1/_2$ cup chopped walnuts

Mix crumbled wafers and margarine. Press into deep 10 inch pie pan. Bake 8 minutes at 375 degrees. Cool.

Melt chocolate bits and marshmallows mixed with evaporated milk. Cool.

Soften ice cream. Spoon $^1/_2$ qt. in crust, cover with half of chocolate mixture. Repeat procedure. Top with chopped walnuts.

Place in freezer until ready to serve. Wrap in sealing wrap after pie is frozen. Place in freezer until ready to serve.

Excellent!
This recipe has been passed around everywhere because it is a favorite. On a scale of 1 to 10, it rates a 12.

pies

layered ice cream pie   serves 12

1¼   cups crushed Chocolate Wafers
3   Tbsp. margarine, melted
       caramel sauce (see recipe)
1   qt. chocolate ice cream, softened
1   qt. vanilla ice cream, softened
6   (1.4 oz) Heath bars or toffee-flavored candy bars, crushed
       chocolate sauce (see recipe)
1   qt. coffee ice cream, softened

Mix crumbled wafers and margarine. Press firmly over bottom of 10 inch springform pan. Bake at 350 degrees for 8 mintues. Cool on wire rack.

Spread caramel sauce over cooled crust; leave a 1 inch border and freeze until set. Spread chocolate ice cream over caramel sauce; freeze until firm.

Combine vanilla ice cream and crushed candy bars. Spread over chocolate ice cream; freeze until firm. Spread enough chocolate sauce to cover; freeze until firm. Spread coffee ice cream as final layer. Return to freezer until set then cover tightly with plastic wrap and freeze for at least 8 hours.

Remove from freezer about 10 minutes before serving, remove springform pan sides, and slice into 12 wedges. If desired serve with remaining sauces. Serve only to those who truly appreciate dessert and won't complain about calories.

For a lower fat-calorie dessert, substitute low-fat margarine in crust, fat-free caramel and chocolate sauces, low-fat or fat-free frozen yogurt, and decrease candy bars to 3.

pies

caramel sauce makes 2 cups

$1/_3$	cup butter
2	cups firmly packed brown sugar
$1/_8$	tsp. salt
1	cup half and half
2	tsp. cornstarch
2	tsp. vanilla extract

Combine butter, sugar, salt and $3/_4$ cup milk in top of double boiler. Cook, stirring constantly until sugar dissolves. Combine cornstarch and remaining milk; gradually stir into sugar mixture. Continue to cook until sauce thickens, stirring frequently. Stir in vanilla.

chocolate sauce makes 1 cup

1	cup chocolate semi-sweet bits
$2/_3$	cup miniature marshmallows
1	($5^3/_4$ oz.) can evaporated milk

Combine all ingredients in saucepan and melt. Cool.

pies

peanut butter pie

1	9 inch deep dish pastry, baked
$^1/_3$	cup peanut butter
$^1/_2$	cup confectioners sugar
$^1/_3$	cup flour
$^1/_2$	cup sugar
$^1/_8$	tsp. salt
2	cups milk
2	egg yolks, slightly beaten
2	tsp. butter
1	tsp. vanilla
8	oz. whipped cream

Mix together peanut butter and confectioners sugar until crumbly. Reserve $^1/_4$ cup mixture and put remainder in baked crust.

Mix together flour, sugar, salt, milk and egg yolks. Bring to a good boil, stirring constantly until thick. Remove from heat.

Add butter and vanilla. Pour into crust and let cool, then cover with whipped cream (slightly sweetened) and sprinkle reserved $^1/_4$ cup mixture on top.

pies

southern pecan pie

3	Tbsp. melted butter
$^1/_2$	cup Light Karo Syrup
3	eggs, beaten
1	tsp. vanilla
	pinch of salt
1	cup sugar
1	cup pecans
	unbaked 9 inch pie crust

Melt butter and add all ingredients except pecans. Mix well and add pecans. Pour into unbaked crust.

Bake in preheated 350 degree oven for 45 minutes or until knife inserted halfway between the outside and center of filling comes out clean. Cool on rack.

pies

caramel coconut pie   makes 2 pies

$^1/_4$ cup margarine*
7   oz. flaked coconut
$^1/_2$ cup chopped pecans
8   oz. cream cheese, softened*
1   14 oz. can sweetened condensed milk*
16   oz. Cool Whip, thawed*
2   baked 9 inch deep dish pie shells
1   12 oz. jar of caramel or butterscotch sauce*

Melt margarine in a non-stick skillet; add coconut and pecans. Stirring frequently, cook until golden brown; cool.

Combine cream cheese and milk; beat with electric mixer on medium speed until smooth. Fold in Cool Whip.

Layer $^1/_4$ of cream cheese mixture in each pastry shell. Drizzle $^1/_4$ of caramel topping over each pie and sprinkle $^1/_4$ of coconut mixture evenly over top. Repeat layers with remaining cream cheese mixture, caramel sauce, and coconut mixture. Cover and freeze pies for 8 hours. Let frozen pies stand at room temperature 5 minutes before slicing.

This pie is one of the all-time best and so easy to make!

*It can be prepared with fewer fat and calories by substituting low-fat margarine, low or fat-free cream cheese, skimmed sweetened condensed milk, light whipped topping, and fat-free caramel sauce (Smucker's is very good). A graham cracker crust made with low or fat-free margarine could be substituted for the pie pastry. Sorry, there's no substitute for the coconut and pecans!

 source: Ann Summers

buttermilk pie

2   sticks butter, melted and cooled
1   cup sugar
$^1/_2$ cup flour
3   eggs
1   cup buttermilk
1   tsp. vanilla

Mix butter, sugar, and flour together. Stir in eggs one at a time and add buttermilk; add vanilla last.

Pour in unbaked 9 inch pie shell. Bake in preheated 325 degree oven for 25 to 30 minutes or until top is set and knife inserted into center comes out clean.

 source: Vivian Obie

pies

pumpkin pie   makes 2 pies

2	unbaked 9 inch deep dish pie crusts
4	eggs
1	29 oz. can of solid packed pumpkin
$1^1/_2$	cups sugar
1	tsp. salt
2	tsp. ground cinnamon
$1^1/_2$	tsp ground ginger
$^1/_2$	tsp. cloves
2	12 oz. cans evaporated milk*

Preheated oven to 425 degrees and prepare crusts.

Lightly beat eggs and stir in remaining ingredients in order given. Pour into unbaked pie crust. If using metal or foil pans, place on preheated heavy duty baking sheet. To avoid spillage when transferring pies to oven, add last cup of filling after placing pies on rack in oven.

Bake for 15 minutes at 425 degres. Reduce temperature to 350 degrees and bake for 40 to 50 minutes or until knife inserted in center comes out clean. Cool on wire rack.

If desired, add Brown Sugar Walnut Topping. (see recipe this section)

*For a lower fat-calories pie, substitute skimmed or low-fat evaporated milk.

pies

mincemeat makes 7 quarts

2	lbs. lean beef chunks	2	lbs. brown sugar
1	Tbsp. salt and pepper	3	pints apple cider
	water	2	Tbsp. cinnamon
1	lb beef suet	1	Tbsp. nutmeg
5	lbs. York or Stayman apples, peeled and sliced	1	Tbsp. cloves
$^1/_2$	lb. citron	1	Tbsp. allspice
$2^1/_2$	lbs. seedless raisins		juice of 2 lemons
2	lbs. currents		

Season beef chunks with salt and pepper. Cover with water and simmer until tender. Cool.

Coarsely grind cooked beef, suet, apple slices and citron. Combine remaining ingredients and mix thoroughly. Pack tightly in sterilized jars. Refrigerate and use as needed. May be stored up to 6 months.

The mincemeat making is still supervised by Mother, who is very exact about her recipe and ingredients used. She allows at least 4 weeks for the mincemeat, sealed and refrigerated, to age before using. - Michael DiGrassie

pies

 # mincemeat pie

2¹/₂   cups mincemeat
       double pastry for 9 inch deep dish pie

Spoon mincemeat into unbaked pie shell. Cover with top crust which
has been vented to allow steam to escape. Bake at 375 to 400
degrees for 30 to 35 minutes. Remove from oven and brush with
melted butter. Place on rack for cooling.

Excellent with Hot Rum Custard Sauce

hot rum custard sauce

1¹/₂   cups milk
1   cup sugar
3   eggs, slightly beaten
1   Tbsp. butter
2-3   Tbsp. cornstarch
2   Tbsp. light rum or rum extract to taste

Heat milk, make paste with sugar, eggs, butter, and cornstarch.
Gradually add paste to hot milk, stirring constantly.

Cook over low heat until thick. Add rum or rum flavoring last. If too
thick, add more milk.

Flavor to suit your personal taste and habit. Light rum gives best
flavor but rum extract is also good. Good on mincemeat and apple pie.

pies

strawberry rhubarb pie

$1^1/_2$	cups sugar
$^1/_4$	cup flour
$^1/_4$	tsp. salt
$^1/_4$	tsp. nutmeg
3	cups $^1/_2$ inch pieces rhubarb
1	cup sliced strawberries
	pastry for a double 9 inch crust
2	Tbsp. butter, cut into small pieces
2	Tbsp. butter, melted

Combine dry ingredients. Add fruit, mix well and let stand 20 minutes. Spoon into pie crust. Dot with butter and moisten crust edge. Add top crust, adjust and flute edge. Cut slits in top to allow steam to escape.

Bake in preheated 400 degree oven about 40 to 50 minutes or until golden brown. Remove from oven and brush with melted butter and cool on wire rack. Serve warm with whipped cream or ice cream.

pies

blackberry cobbler

3	cups sugar
3	quarts fresh or frozen blackberries
1	stick margarine
	water
4-5	Tbsp. cornstarch
	unbaked pastry for single crust

Bring sugar, blackberries, and margarine to boil. Add enough water to cornstarch to make smooth paste. Remove berries from heat; add thickening gradually, stirring constantly. Return to heat and cook until thickened.

Prepare crust. Pour thickened berries into buttered 8x8 inch pan. Cover with pie pastry, seal the edges of the pastry to the pan. Cut several slits in top of crust to vent, brush with melted butter or margarine, and bake at 350 degrees for 30 to 40 minutes or until golden brown.

pies

fresh peach pie

	pastry for 9 inch double pie crust
5	cups fresh peaches, peeled and sliced
$1^1/_2$	tsp. lemon juice
1	cup sugar
$^1/_4$	cup flour
$^1/_2$	tsp. ground cinnamon
$^1/_8$	tsp. nutmeg
2	Tbsp. butter, cut into small bits

Preheat oven to 425 degrees. Prepare bottom crust in 9 inch pie pan. Set aside pastry for top crust.

Gently toss peaches with lemon juice; set aside. Combine dry ingredients and sprinkle over peaches. Spoon peaches evenly into pie crust and moisten edges of crust with water. Prepare pastry for top crust, place over pie, crimp edges, and cut vents in top for steam too escape. Bake in preheated oven for 35 to 40 minutes or until golden brown. If edges begin to brown before the remainder of the pie, cover edges with foil. Remove from oven, brush with melted butter and cool on wire rack.

pies

plain pastry makes two 9 or 10 inch crusts

2   cups all purpose flour
1   tsp. salt
$^2/_3$ cup shortening
5-7   Tbsp. cold milk

Sift together flour and salt. Cut in shortening with pastry blender or fork until pieces are the size of small peas. Sprinkle 1 Tbsp. milk over part of mixture. Gently toss with fork and push to side of bowl. Sprinkle next Tbsp of milk over dry part. Mix lightly and push to moistened part at side. Repeat until all is moistened. Form into ball.

Divide dough into two balls. Flatten ball slightly and roll $^1/_8$ inch thick on lightly floured surface.

Always use a light touch and handle dough as little as possible.

Homeade pie crusts are wonderful if you have the time to make them, however there are prepared refrigerated or frozen crusts which are very good. A few good ones are Pillsbury refrigerated crusts and Rich's and Kroger's frozen crusts.

pies

vinegar pie crust   makes two 9 inch crusts

2   cups sifted flour
$^1/_2$ tsp. salt
$1^1/_2$ tsp. vinegar
1   cup plus 1 Tbsp. Crisco
1   egg, beaten
5   Tbsp. ice water or just enough to mix dough

Mix all ingredients together and shape into 2 balls. Roll out on lightly floured board. If baking a single crust, bake at 400 degrees for 10 minutes.

Will keep in refrigerator for 2 weeks.

meringue

4	room temperature egg whites
$1/4$	tsp. cream of tartar
3	Tbsp. sugar

Add cream of tartar to egg whites, beat until almost stiff enough to hold peak, add sugar gradually. Beat until stiff but not dry.

Pile lightly on pie filling, sealing edges. Bake in slow oven at 325 degrees until lightly browned.

<u>To prevent weeping</u>
Add sugar 1 Tbsp. at a time and thoroughly beat after each.
Seal edges of meringue over crust. Always bake in slow oven.

weepless meringue   covers 8 or 9 inch pie

1	Tbsp. cornstarch	3	egg whites
2	Tbsp. sugar		dash of salt
$1/2$	cup hot water	6	Tbsp. sugar

Combine cornstarch and 2 Tbsp. sugar. Stir in water and cook over low heat until thickend and clear, stirring constantly. Cool.
Whip egg whites and salt until soft peaks form. Beat cornstarch mixture and 6 Tbsp. sugar into whites, beating well after each addition. Beat until creamy. Pile on pie and bake 30 minutes at 325 degrees or until golden brown.

 source: Virginia Craft Bowers

pies

other great desserts

boiled custard serve as a dessert

4   egg yolks
$^1/_4$ cup sugar
3   cups milk, scalded
        pinch salt
1   Tbsp. vanilla

Beat yolks and sugar lightly. Add scalded milk. Pour into double boiler over low heat, stirring constantly. Continue stirring and cooking until custard coats a spoon. Remove from heat and add vanilla.

Sprinkle freshly grated nutmeg on top. Store in refrigerator.

If mixture curdles, remove from heat and beat with a rotary beater until smooth.

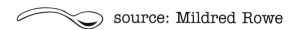 source: Mildred Rowe

It wouldn't be Christmas without Mother's boiled custard and fresh coconut cake. I spent my first Christmas away from home in 1972. I was living in California and was faced with a sunny warm Christmas without family or Mother's custard. I telephoned home for the recipe. Her first words were "Go out and buy a glass double boiler. It must be glass." I scoured San Diego and finally found one. I made the custard but it wasn't as good as Mother's. That was the first, last and only Christmas away from home. - Linda Hanna

lemon pudding

1	qt. milk
1	Tbsp. butter
$1^3/_4$	cups sugar
3	Tbsp. cornstarch
	milk
4	egg yolks
$1^1/_2$	Tbsp pure lemon extract

Heat milk and butter in double boiler. Mix sugar and corn starch and a small amount of milk to make a smooth paste. Add egg yolks and mix thoroughly. Pour into hot milk, stirring constantly. Allow to thicken and add lemon extract to taste.

Remove from heat and serve warm.

banana pudding

4	cups milk	1	heaping Tbsp. butter
4	egg yolks (reserve whites)		Vanilla wafers
4	Tbsp. cornstarch	3-4	firm bananas
$^3/_4$	cup sugar		lemon juice
	water		meringue (see Mrs. Rowe's
2	tsp. vanilla		Meringue Recipe)

Place milk in double boiler and heat.

In bowl, stir together egg yolks, cornstarch and sugar. Add just enough water to make a soupy paste. Add this mixture gradually to hot milk. Stir constantly and away from the sides. Stir and cook until a pudding consistency. Remove from heat, stir in vanilla and butter.

Layer pan or dish with vanilla wafers, sliced bananas and pudding. Top with meringue. Bake in 325 degree oven until brown, 20 to 30 minutes.

You may omit the meringue and top with coarsely crumbled vanilla wafers. No baking required.

Prepare a mixture of 2 parts of lemon juice to 1 part water to coat banana slices to prevent them from turning dark.

 source: Vivian Obie, Baker, Mrs. Rowe's

bread pudding with raisin sauce

5	cups coarsely ground bread	2	tsp. vanilla
5	eggs	$^1/_2$	tsp. nutmeg
2	cups sugar	2	Tbsp. melted butter
3	cups milk		

Place ground bread in buttered baking dish. Mix remaining ingredients together and pour over bread. Sprinkle with nutmeg. Bake in preheated 350 degree oven for 55 to 65 minutes or golden brown. Brush top with melted butter and serve warm with Raisin or Lemon Sauce.

This is best made with day old rolls which are coarsely ground, however you may use day old sliced bread, 8 to 10 slices torn into pieces.

raisin sauce

1	cup raisins	2	Tbsp. butter
3	cups water	$^1/_2$	tsp. nutmeg
1	cup sugar	3	Tbsp. cornstarch
2	Tbsp. fresh lemon juice	$^1/_4$	cup water
	pinch of salt		

Soak raisins in water for 30 minutes to 1 hour.

Drain raisins and save water. Place water in saucepan. Add sugar, lemon juice, butter, salt and nutmeg. Stir and heat until dissolved. Mix cornstarch and water. Add slowly to mixture. When desired consistency, add raisins.

 source: Vivian Obie, Baker, Mrs. Rowe's

pineapple bread pudding

2	qts. day-old firm textured bread
$1/_2$	cup margarine, melted
$1/_2$	cup pineapple juice
2	cups crushed pineapple, drained
$1^1/_4$	cups raisins
3	eggs
$3/_4$	cup firmly packed brown sugar
$1/_4$	tsp. cinnamon
$1/_4$	tsp. nutmeg
$1/_8$	tsp. allspice
1	cup milk

Tear or cut bread into 1 inch pieces and place in a buttered baking pan. Drizzle with margarine, then pineapple juice to moisten evenly. Sprinkle pineapple and raisins over bread and mix lightly.

Beat eggs with brown sugar and spices; stir in milk. Pour evenly over ingredients in baking pan. Bake in preheated 350 degree oven for about 40 minutes or until custard is set in center of pan. Serve with warm Vanilla Custard Sauce.

vanilla custard sauce

$1^1/_2$	cups milk
1	cup sugar
3	eggs, slightly beaten
1	Tbsp. butter, melted
3	Tbsp. cornstarch
1	tsp. vanilla

In double boiler, heat milk. Make paste with sugar, eggs, butter and cornstarch. Stirring constantly, gradually add paste to hot milk and cook until thick. Add vanilla last. If too thick, add more milk. Serve warm.

rice pudding

1	cup cooked rice
$1/_2$	cup sugar
$1/_2$	cup raisins
$2^1/_2$	cups milk
1	tsp. lemon or vanilla extract
$1/_4$	tsp. nutmeg
4	eggs

Mix together and pour into buttered baking dish. Bake at preheated 350 degree oven for 15 minutes. Reduce temperature to 325 degree and continue to bake until set, about 40 to 45 minutes. Good served warm but allow some cooling time.

Great way to use leftover rice. When cooking fresh rice, cut down on starch by washing the rice and begin cooking in cold water.

So quick and easy. To save additional time, use rice which has been previously cooked, divided into 1 cup portions and frozen.

blueberry crisp

3	cups fresh or fresh frozen blueberries
$^3/_4$	cup sugar
$^1/_4$	cup water*
$^1/_4$	cup cornstarch

Wash and drain blueberries; in medium saucepan combine berries, sugar, and water. Bring to a boil; add small amount of water to cornstarch to make a paste and add to blueberry mixture. Simmer until thickened. Pour into a buttered 8x8 inch baking dish. Cover with brown sugar topping and bake in a preheated 450 degree oven about 20 minutes or until browned and bubbly. Serve warm with whipped cream or vanilla ice cream and blueberry sauce. *may need to adjust water

topping
$^1/_2$	cup brown sugar
2	cups homemade ground bread crumbs
$^1/_2$	stick butter or margarine, melted

Combine sugar and bread crumbs. Add butter and mix.

blueberry sauce
Reserve 1/2 cup of blueberry mixture. Add $^1/_2$ cup water to thin and simmer for a few minutes. Keep warm and serve over the scoop of ice cream on the blueberry crisp.

 source: Richard Bell, Baker, Mrs. Rowe's

apple brown betty

$3^1/_2$	lb. canned apples or 8 to 10 cups fresh peeled, sliced York or Stayman apples
2	cups sugar
$^1/_2$	cup raisins
$^1/_2$	Tbsp. nutmeg, to taste
$^1/_2$	Tbsp. cinnamon, to taste
$1^1/_2$	Tbsp. cornstarch
$^1/_4$	cup water

Bring apples, sugar, raisins, nutmeg and cinnamon to a boil. Add thickening of cornstarch and water to the apple mixture. Simmer until thickened. Pour into buttered 9x13 inch pan. Add topping and bake in 450 degree oven for 30 minutes or until golden brown.

Wonderful served with whipped cream, ice cream or Lemon Sauce (see recipe).

topping
$^3/_4$	cup firmly packed light brown sugar
3	cups finely ground bread crumbs, homemade preferred
$^3/_4$	stick butter, melted

Mix brown sugar with bread crumbs. Add butter and mix.

apple dumplings   makes 4 large dumplings

4   large, tart apples, peeled and cored
$^1/_2$ cup sugar
$1^1/_2$ tsp. cinnamon
2   tsp. butter

<u>pastry</u>   <u>sauce</u>
2   cups flour $^2/_3$ cup sugar
1   tsp. salt $1^1/_2$ cups water
$^3/_4$ cup Crisco, plus 2 Tbsp. 2   Tbsp. butter
$^1/_4$ cup ice water $^1/_4$ tsp. cinnamon

Mix together $^1/_2$ cup sugar and $1^1/_2$ tsp. cinnamon and set aside.

Combine sugar, water, butter and cinnamon; bring to boil. Boil for 3 minutes to make sauce and set aside.

Sift together flour and salt. Add Crisco and just enough water to hold flour together. Use hands, rather than pastry cutter or fork, to mix. Be careful not to knead dough too much or the pastry will be tough. Divide into four balls, roll out on lightly floured surface, and shape into squares. Place whole apple in each pastry square.

Fill each apple cavity with cinnamon-sugar mixture. Lightly moisten edges of the square. Fold the corners to the center and pinch the edges together. Dot each top with $^1/_2$ tsp. butter and place the apples in buttered baking dish with 1 cup sauce in the bottom. Bake in preheated oven at 375 degrees for 20 minutes. Remove from oven and add remainder of sauce and baste. (Make sure that baking dish is large enough to allow room for basting the apples.) Return to oven and bake approximately 30 minutes longer or until golden brown. Baste several times during final baking.

Use a tart apple such as Rambo, York, or Stayman.

This recipe will make 4 large or six small apple dumplings. Serve warm with pure cream or ice cream. Cinnamon ice cream is especially good on this dessert.

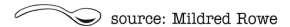 source: Mildred Rowe

When Mother makes Apple Dumplings, usually in the fall when the apples are the best, she makes about 2 dozen or more at a time and shares with anyone who happens to drop by. I've sampled a lot of apple dumplings but none quite like hers. The secret is the perfect apple and her wonderful pastry. - Brenda Hathaway

baked apple roll-ups   serves 10

$1^1/_2$ cups sugar
2   cups water
$^1/_2$ tsp. cinnamon
1   stick margarine or butter
5   cups peeled and chopped apples (about 6 large apples)
2   tsp. ground cinnamon
10   (6 inch) flour tortillas
        ice cream or whipped cream

Combine sugar, $^1/_2$ tsp. cinnamon, and water in saucepan to make sauce; cook over medium heat, stirring constantly, until sugar melts. Set aside.

Melt butter in a 13x9x2 inch baking dish and set aside. Combine and stir to coat chopped apples and cinnamon.

Place $^1/_2$ cup apple mixture down center of each tortilla. Fold, with sides overlapping and place seam side down in baking dish. The rolls must fit close together in order to fit ten in the dish but this is as it should be. Pour the sauce over the top of the filled tortillas and cover with aluminum foil.

Bake at 350 degrees for 30 minutes. Remove foil, baste with sauce and return to oven. Bake an additional 30 minutes, basting twice during the final baking period. Serve warm with ice cream or whipped cream.

If you prefer a large portion of the roll-up, buy the 8 inch flour tortilla and fill with just less than 1 cup apples. Makes about 6 large tortillas.

Could serve with a mexican theme dinner and call it mexican apple pie.

gingerbread

$1/2$	cup boiling water
$1/2$	cup butter or margarine
$1/2$	cup light brown sugar
$1/2$	cup dark molasses
2	eggs
$1 1/4$	cups flour
$1/2$	tsp. salt
$3/4$	tsp. baking soda
$1/2$	tsp. ginger
$1/2$	tsp. cinnamon
$1/2$	tsp. nutmeg

Combine butter, sugar, and molasses and pour the boiling water over. Stir until butter is melted. Set aside to cool, then beat in the eggs. Sift flour, salt, soda, and spices together; then stir into the liquid mixture. Beat until smooth and pour into a buttered 8x8 inch baking pan. Bake in 325 degree oven for 50 minutes or until done. Serve with Old Fashioned Lemon Sauce or Lemon Custard Sauce. (see recipe)

old fashioned lemon sauce

2	Tbsp. conrstarch	1	egg yolk
$^1/_2$	cup sugar	1	Tbsp. cold water
2	cups cold water	3	Tbsp. lemon juice
2	Tbsp. butter, softened	1	tsp. grated lemon peel

Combine cornstarch and sugar in saucepan; stir in 2 cups cold water. Cook, stirring constantly over medium-low heat until very thick. Add butter; stir until blended. Beat egg yolk with 1 Tbsp. water. Stir a small amount of hot mixture into egg yolk-water combination, then add egg mixture to the saucepan. Stirring constantly, cook 1 to 2 minutes. Do NOT Boil. Remove from heat and stir in lemon juice and grated peel. Serve warm.

lemon custard sauce

$2^1/_2$	cups milk		milk
$1^1/_2$	tsp. butter	2	egg yolks
$^3/_4$	cup plus 2 Tbsp. sugar	2	tsp. pure lemon extract
$1^1/_2$	Tbsp. cornstarch		

Heat milk and butter in doubleboiler. Make smooth paste with sugar, cornstarch and milk. Add egg yolks and mix thoroughly. Pour into hot milk, stirring constantly. Allow to thicken and add lemon extract to taste. Adjust amount of milk for desired consistency. Remove from heat and serve warm.

oatmeal raisin cookies

1	cup Butter Flavor Crisco
1	cup granulated sugar
3	eggs
$^1/_4$	cup molasses
2	cups all-purpose flour
2	cups quick cooking rolled oats
$^1/_2$	tsp. salt
$^1/_2$	tsp. cinnamon
1	tsp. baking soda
$1^1/_2$	cups raisins

Preheat oven to 375 degrees. Cream shortening; add sugar, eggs, and molasses. Beat well. Add flour, oats, salt, cinnamon, and soda. Blend well. Fold in raisins.

Drop by rounded Tbsp. onto greased cookie sheet. Bake for 10 to 12 minutes or until cookie is lightly browned. Remove from cookie sheet and cool on wire rack.

pecan chocolate chunk cookies makes 6 dozen

1	cup butter or margarine, softened
$3/_4$	cup sugar
$3/_4$	cup firmly packed brown sugar
1	tsp. vanilla
2	eggs
$2^1/_4$	cups flour
1	tsp. baking soda
$1/_2$	tsp. salt
24	oz. semi-sweet baking chunks, chopped or jumbo chips
1	cup coarsely chopped peanuts

Cream together butter and sugars; add vanilla and eggs, beating well. Combine flour, baking soda, and salt. Slowly add dry ingredients to butter mixture. Stir in chocolate and nuts.

Drop by rounded teaspoonsfuls onto ungreased baking sheet. Bake in preheated 375 degree oven for 9 or 10 minutes or until lightly browned. Cool on wire rack.

old fashioned sugar cookies

1	cup shortening
2	cups sugar, divided
2	eggs
1	tsp. lemon extract
1	tsp. vanilla
$2^1/_2$	cups all purpose flour
2	tsp. baking powder
$^1/_4$	tsp. salt

Cream shortening, add $1^1/_2$ cups sugar and beat until fluffy. Add eggs and flavoring, mixing well. Combine flour, baking powder and salt. Add to creamed mixture and blend well.

Drop dough by heaping Tbsp. full 3 inches apart onto greased cookie sheet. Press cookie with fork to flatten. Sprinkle cookies with remainder of sugar.

Bake at 375 degrees for 10 minutes or until lightly brown.

orange blossoms

the juice and grated peel of 2 oranges
the juice and grated peel of 2 lemons
$1^1/_4$ box 10X sugar
$1^1/_2$ cups flour
$1^1/_2$ tsp. baking powder
$^1/_2$ tsp. salt
3 eggs
$^1/_2$ cup water
1 tsp. vanilla
$1^1/_3$ cups white sugar

Mix juices. Add peel and 10X sugar. Mix well. Make the day before if desired and refrigerate. Be sure to stir well before using.

Sift together flour, baking powder and salt.

Beat eggs. Add water, vanilla and sugar. Mix well. Add flour, baking powder and salt. Mix. Butter miniature muffin tins and fill $^3/_4$ full of batter. Bake 10 minutes at 350 degrees. While still warm, dip in juice mixture. Drain on foil or waxed paper.

Favorite of everyone.

lemon squares

1	cup flour
1	stick butter
$1/4$	cup 10X sugar
2	eggs, slightly beaten
$1/2$	tsp. baking poweder
2	Tbsp. flour
1	cup sugar
3	Tbsp. fresh lemon juice

Mix together flour, butter and 10X sugar. Press into bottom of a greased 9 inch square pan. Bake at 350 degrees for 20 minutes.

Mix together remaining ingredients. Pour in top of crust and bake 25 minutes at 350 degrees. Sift powdered sugar on top.

peanut butter chocolate brownies

makes 24 squares

	vegetable cooking spray
1	cup flour
1	tsp. baking powder
$1/4$	tsp. salt
$1/2$	cup peanut butter
$1/3$	cup margarine, softened
$1/2$	cup granulated sugar
$1/2$	cup firmly packed brown sugar
2	eggs
1	tsp. vanilla
6	oz. semisweet chocolate chips

Spray 8x8 inch baking pan with cooking spray. Preheat oven to 350 degrees. Mix together flour, baking powder and salt; set aside.

With electric beaters on medium speed, cream peanut butter, margarine, and sugars until smooth and fluffy. Beat in eggs and vanilla until blended. Add dry ingredients and stir just until combined. Stir in chocolate chips.

Evenly spread in pan, bake about 30 to 35 minutes. Do not overbake. Cool in pan on wire rack and cut into squares.

 source: Anne Wilson Finley

miscellaneous

miscellaneous

sweetened tea

In the South, cold sweetened tea is a staple. It's made by the gallon, sweetened, refrigerated, and always available. Especially in the Carolinas, sweetened tea is served in the restaurants, so it's always best to taste before adding sugar or sweetener.

Before beginning, you need a gallon jar for storing tea and a container which boiling water can be poured into for steeping tea.

1	gallon water
16	single or 4 family size tea bags
9	grains saccarin
1	cup sugar

Boil water. Put sugar in gallon jar and saccharin in container for steeping tea; set aside. Twist strings of tea bags and place into steeping container so that they will hang together with ends on the outside. Hold teabags securely while pouring boiling water over; cover, let steep for 15 minutes and pour into gallon jar. Repeat the process of pouring boiling water over tea bags until all water has been used. Serve with lots of ice and a big wedge of lemon.

Sugar and saccharin should be adjusted according to personal preference or if unsweetened tea is desired, omit the sweeteners. Tea can be refrigerated for several days

miscellaneous

party tea

Pour 5 cups boiling water over 5 individual tea bags. Steep for 5 minutes. Add 5 cups of cold water and $^3/_4$ to 1 cup of sugar (may subsititute part with saccarin). Add one 6 oz. can of frozen limeade and mix well. Garnish with fresh mint.

 source: Janet Ferguson

Russian tea mix

$^1/_2$	cup instant tea	Mix together and store tightly sealed. Use 2 heaping tsp. to one cup boiling water.
$^1/_2$	cup sugar	
1	tsp. ground cinnamon	
$^1/_2$	tsp. ground cloves	
1	large (1 lb. 2 oz.) jar Tang	Great gift for giving with recipe attached.
1	small package lemonade mix	

spicy tea   makes 12 servings

2	qts. boiling water	Pour boiling water over tea, allspice, and lemon rind. Cover and let stand for 5 minutes. Strain into hot teapot. Garnish with lemon slices. Sweeten if desired.
12	teabags or $^1/_2$ cup loose tea	
1	tsp. cracked allspice	
	rind of 1 lemon	
	thinly sliced lemons	

basic white sauce

THIN: makes $1^1/_2$ cups
1   Tbsp. butter
1   Tbsp. flour
$^1/_4$ tsp. salt
$1^1/_2$ cups milk

Melt butter in saucepan over low heat. Blend in flour, salt, and dash of white pepper. Add milk, cook quickly, stirring constantly, until mixture is thick and bubbles. Good for soups and creamed vegetables.

MEDIUM: makes 1 cup
2   Tbsp. butter
2   Tbsp. flour
$^1/_4$ tsp. salt
1   cup milk
Good for sauces, creamed and scalloped dishes. Creamed chipped beef on biscuits, creamed fresh asparagus, mushrooms or eggs on toast points.

THICK: makes 1 cup
3   Tbsp. butter
4   Tbsp. flour
$^1/_4$ tsp. salt
1   cup milk

Sauces for croquettes, salmon cakes.

Rowe's Family Restaurant
74 Rowe Road
Staunton, VA 24401

"Mrs. Rowe's Favorite Recipes"

The collection includes the best that our kitchen has served over the years. In addition, many are long-time favorites of Mrs. Rowe and family members. Some are original, some are shared by good friends, some from long-lost sources, and some handed down from generation to generation.

PLEASE SEND ME _____ COPIES OF "ROWE'S RECIPES" AT $12.95* EACH, PLUS $2.00 SHIPPING AND HANDLING (PER BOOK). VA RESIDENTS ADD 4.5% SALES TAX.

TOTAL: $_____

☐ CHECK ENCLOSED   CHARGE TO: ☐ VISA   ☐ MASTERCARD

CARDHOLDER'S NAME _____

CARD # _____ EXP. DATE _____ / _____

CARDHOLDER'S SIGNATURE _____

SEND TO:
NAME: _____

ADDRESS:_____

CITY: _____

STATE:_____ ZIP: _____

*PRICE OF BOOK SUBJECT TO CHANGE

- -

Rowe's Family Restaurant
74 Rowe Road
Staunton, VA 24401

"Mrs. Rowe's Favorite Recipes"

The collection includes the best that our kitchen has served over the years. In addition, many are long-time favorites of Mrs. Rowe and family members. Some are original, some are shared by good friends, some from long-lost sources, and some handed down from generation to generation.

PLEASE SEND ME _____ COPIES OF "ROWE'S RECIPES" AT $12.95* EACH, PLUS $2.00 SHIPPING AND HANDLING (PER BOOK). VA RESIDENTS ADD 4.5% SALES TAX.

TOTAL: $_____

☐ CHECK ENCLOSED   CHARGE TO: ☐ VISA   ☐ MASTERCARD

CARDHOLDER'S NAME _____

CARD # _____ EXP. DATE _____ / _____

CARDHOLDER'S SIGNATURE _____

SEND TO:
NAME: _____

ADDRESS:_____

CITY: _____

STATE:_____ ZIP: _____

*PRICE OF BOOK SUBJECT TO CHANGE